The
Peasant
Venture

The Peasant Venture

Tradition, Migration, and Change among
Georgian Peasants in Turkey

PAUL J. MAGNARELLA

with contributions by
AHMET OZKAN

G.K.HALL &CO.

BOSTON, MASS.

SCHENKMAN PUBLISHING COMPANY
CAMBRIDGE, MASSACHUSETTS

Library of Congress Cataloging in Publication Data

Magnarella, Paul J
  The peasant venture.

    1. Peasantry—Turkey—Case studies. 2. Rural-
urban migration—Europe—Case studies. 3. Alien
labor—Europe—Case studies. I. Title.
HD1513.T9M33 1978   301.44'43'09561   78-13517
ISBN 0-8161-8271-X (cloth)

This publication is printed on permanent/durable acid-free paper
MANUACTURED IN THE UNITED STATES OF AMERICA

Contents

Acknowledgements

With sincere appreciation, I take this opportunity to acknowledge some of the many kind people who contributed to the research, writing, and publication of this book. Dr. John Drake and Dr. William Haviland of the University of Vermont, Dr. James Pierson of California State College — San Bernadino, Dr. Lindsay Pratt of Erskine College, and two anonymous prepublication reviewers read various sections of the manuscript and offered constructive suggestions. Dr. Gardiner Barnum of the University of Vermont supplied technical advice on the book's maps and figures; Mrs. Fusun Tiregol Floyd helped with problems of Turkish translation; and Dr. Arnold Leder of Southwest Texas State University offered helpful suggestions for the section on politics and government. Ahmet Ozkan not only made important contributions to the book's contents, but he along with his gracious family and relatives made the study possible and pleasurable. My wife, Sharlene, helped catch many of my misspellings and typographical errors in the galleys, while Alfred S. Schenkman again proved to be a most understanding publisher. To all of them, thank you.

Financial support for the study was provided, in part, by a Harvard University Sinclair Kennedy Travelling Fellowship and a University of Vermont Summer Faculty Fellowship. I am grateful to these institutions for their support.

The noble people of Hayriye offered me their hospitality and friendship. They are certainly among the most gracious people I have ever met anywhere, and it is to them that this book is dedicated.

Paul J. Magnarella
August, 1978
Burlington, Vermont

Note on Exchange Rate

From 1961 to the official rates of exchange in Turkey were as follows: 1961-1969, TL9.00 = $1.00; 1970, TL15.00 = $1.00; 1971-1975, TL14.00 = $1.00.

Note on Turkish Pronunciation

Each Turkish letter possesses one sound value, and most sounds are not foreign to the English language. Some of the major differences between Turkish and English orthography are as follows:

c is pronounced as the *j* in "jar"

ç is pronounced as the *ch* in "chair"

ğ usually is not pronounced and indicates that its preceeding vowel is lengthened

ı is pronounced as the *u* in "measure"

ö is pronounced as the German *o* in *schon* or the *eu* in the French *deux*

ş is pronounced as the *sh* in "ship"

ü is pronounced as the German *u* in *fur*

The
Peasant
Venture

1
Introduction

Among the many epigraphs created to capture the critical dimensions of our transilient twentieth century, the "Age of Peasant Migration and Mass Urbanization" should certainly be included. Throughout much of human history, peasants have tended to be people of cultural persistence and only marginal participants in either the great classical traditions or the more modern industrial civilizations. In the twentieth century, however, the conditions that maintained this relationship changed dramatically. With the spread of industrial urbanization, the concomitant expansion of industrial markets, and progressively enveloping travel and communication networks, peasants around the world have been succumbing to the power of ideas, values, and models inappropriate to their traditional lifestyles, but inextricable from the mass production, consumption-oriented, industrial societies that bred and nurtured them.

Since their inception, cities have played a prodigious role in the determination of mankind's future. They have been loci of innovation and centers of diffusion. In our century, the generality and intensity of influence

1

emanating from cities have approached global limits. As a consequence, millions of peasants have joined the uprooted, leaving those small communities that constituted the distinctive folk cultures of the earth's many niches to join homogenizing mass societies. As if under the control of a time machine, these peasants collapse a long process of historical development into the short time interval necessary to move from their medieval villages to modernizing metropolises. In another brief period, they must develop new social norms and cultural patterns so as to adapt successfully to their new milieu. They have been emancipated from the soil, but captivated by a modern dream. As Lopreato (1967:xiii) has succinctly written, these "peasants want to be peasants no more."

This present work addresses the complicated topic of peasant mobility and change. In particular, it deals with peasant emigration from a Muslim community in Turkey across state and cultural boundaries to Christian, industrial Europe. It explores the structural and personal reasons for this movement and assesses the consequences for its human participants and their "sending" community. We chose this topic in part because we strongly agree with Erik Cohen's recent statement that social scientists have paid too little attention to the impact of transnational forces on small Middle East communities, even though many of these communities are significantly affected by such forces (Cohen 1977:328).

The book has several major objectives. One is to describe the culture and society of Hayriye, a Muslim Georgian village in Northwestern Anatolia. Because so little has been written about the lives of Georgians who fled their Caucasian homeland in the late nineteenth century, the achievement of this first objective alone would constitute a contribution. The book's second goal involves the analysis of recent emigration from Hayriye to Europe. This aspect of the book constitutes a study of the village in its midstream transition from a local, peasant orientation to an urban national and international orientation. The third objective is the formulation and application of a "model of man in change," which is intended both to explain the psychosocial and cultural dimensions of emigration in this particular case and to constitute a modest contribution to theories of change involving peasants and other "modernizing" peoples.

Several major sources have contributed information to this study. Ahmet Ozkan (Melashvili), a Georgian architect and a Turkish citizen, has worked in Hayriye as a self-appointed development enthusiast since 1960. In addition to divising plans to improve the village's economic situation, he was interested in studying and preserving its remaining Georgian culture. Hence, he drew scale diagrams of various items comprising the village's material culture, helped organize a village dance group, and recorded village music, poems, riddles, and songs. He contributed significantly to the ethnographic aspects of this book. In addition to furnishing the plates which carry his initials, he is responsible for an important portion of Chapter VIII. Ahmet Ozkan is also an author in his own right, having published a general work on Georgian culture (in Turkish) in 1968 under the title *Georgia: Culture, Literature, Art, History, Folklore.*

Among Ozkan's many achievements for Hayriye was his success in convincing the faculty of Turkey's Middle East Technical University (METU) to conduct a series of socioeconomic surveys in the village so as to better comprehend its fundamental problems and provide a basis for future planning. The METU faculty had previously decided to study a village each year from one of Turkey's sixteen different regions. They hoped such studies would provide their students and themselves with solid field experience and the opportunity to contribute to a better understanding of Turkey's rural conditions. Thanks to Ozkan's persuasive efforts, they chose Hayriye as the first village in their series. In 1961-62 teams of faculty and students, including engineers, architects, economists, sociologists, and regional planners, descended on Hayriye to conduct research. A comprehensive report of their work appeared in Turkish in mimeograph form in 1963. This report, which will be referred to in the text as the METU study and in text references as *Hayriye Köy Araştırma* [Hayriye Village Research] 1963, provides much of the baseline data for our study.[1] It, along with my own field notes, helps depict conditions in Hayriye before large scale emigration began in 1965.

The third major source of information is my own field research in Hayriye and in other communities of this general region (see Magnarella 1974, 1976). I made field trips to Hayriye in the Spring of 1970 and in the summers of 1972 and 1974. Each time I lived with a local family, participated fairly extensively in their daily round of activities, and interviewed numerous members of the village community. I had already acquired a high proficiency in Turkish and could communicate in that language with anyone in the village, except pre-school children. Thanks to Ahmet Ozkan and the people of Hayriye, I was well received and provided with every kind of assistance and cooperation. Hence, my research was extremely productive. In addition to most of the information conveyed in the text, all of the photographs were taken during these field trips. Other sources of information utilized in this study are referenced throughout the text in their appropriate places.

The book proceeds somewhat deliberately and, I hope, logically. The seven chapters following this introduction function primarily to establish the background to the major topic of emigration by describing elements of village culture and society and tracing their historic development. Chapter II places the subject people of this study—the Georgians of Hayriye—into historic and geographic perspective. Chapter III describes their kinship and social organization and relates the village to its regional and national environment. Chapter IV deals with important elements of the villagers' traditional culture: rites of passage and ethnotherapy. Chapters V and VI describe the village's pre-emigration economy and polity, while Chapter VII deals with education, ethnic identity, and assimilation.

The remaining chapters constitute the book's second part. Chapter VIII describes organizational efforts in the village and large scale emigration to Europe, while Chapter IX analyzes this emigration in terms of our "model of man in change." Chapter X treats those aspects of change which may be considered consequences of emigration, and Chapter XI offers a final assessment of the situation along with some words about the future.

Throughout this work, efforts have been made to deal with this village in its historic, regional, national, and international contexts and to relate experiences observed here to those of similar communities in other parts of the world. Because I believe the subject people of this study can best be classified as "peasants," some explanatory background to this concept is appropriate before embarking on Chapter II.

Peasants

About half of the world's present population can be placed into the complicated sociocultural, economic, and political category known as peasant.[2] Peasants have existed in Europe, Asia, the Middle East, Latin America, the Caribbean, and Africa for centuries. Apparently, they owe their ubiquitous existence to their admirable tolerance for long hours of backbreaking work and low levels of consumption. Although peasantries vary enormously through history and throughout the world, many (but not all) anthropologists are in basic agreement with the following part of Kroeber's (1948:284) early definition of them:

> Peasants are definitely rural—yet live in relation to market towns; they form a class segment of a larger population which usually contains also urban centers, sometimes metropolitan capitals. They constitute part-societies with part-cultures. They lack the isolation, the political autonomy, and the self-sufficiency of tribal populations; but their local units retain much of their old identity...

Further anthropological discussion of peasants has emphasized two sets of relationships: those between the peasant community and the outside world, and those within the community itself.

The first set of relationships corresponds to Kroeber's "part-societies/part-cultures" conceptualization of peasants. Both economically and socially, peasant communities are commonly viewed as the lowest stratum within a large, complex, hierarchically organized state. Most peasants earn their livelihood by subsistence or semi-subsistence agriculture. They are economically tied to urban centers, in that they sell their surplus, if any, in regional markets where they buy those necessary goods they themselves cannot produce. Peasant communities form low-level political-administrative units whose affairs are regulated by higher urban units. In this relationship, peasant communities are usually considered subordinate and impotent. Many anthropologists contend that peasant exploitation is also a universal characteristic of this relationship, however they rarely define exploitation or explain whether its form is unique to peasants (Dalton 1974).

Redfield discussed the "part-cultures" aspect of this relationship quite eloquently. He distinguished two separate, but interdependent levels of culture: the classical "Great Tradition," consisting of the science, philosophy, religion, and fine art of the critical and reflective urban elite, and the "Little Tradition," composed of the technology, lore, religion, and folk art of peasants and other common people (Redfield 1956). An exchange between these two levels occurs, with elements of the Great Tradition more usually diffusing down to peasants who "parochialize" them into their Little Traditions. More recently, Clifford Geertz (1962:2) observed that "most of the rural people commonly referred to as peasants in Western Europe, Japan and much of Latin America stand in a complementary relationship not to a classical great tradition, a bazaar-type market system, or a traditional hereditary elite, but to modern mass culture, highly industrialized economy, and a thoroughly bureaucratized government." Today, this observation applies to the Middle East as well.

Relationships within many peasant communities are frequently characterized by relative sociocultural and economic homogeneity. The elemental organization cells are usually kinship-based households. Typically, each household forms the basic unit of production and consumption, and engages in the same subsistence activities as other households. Consequently, many members of a peasant community share similar socioeconomic circumstances and responses to common problems, although their statuses may vary.

Much of a peasant's life is spent in his village. He or she lives in long association with other villagers and interacts with them in an intimate, face-to-face manner. Villagers share a common fund of knowledge about all their coresidents. Collectively they set standards of conduct and apply sanctions for their maintenance. Much of this can be summed up by saying that the internal organization of peasant communities is structured by sets of "multistranded" relationships (Wolf 1966). This means that peasants interact with familiar others in multiple and overlapping roles involving economic, political, religious, and social content.

In their village, peasants provide each other with a sense of identity vis-à-vis the outside. Despite its part-society/part-culture nature, each peasant community is like a world apart: one of the many unique and small components, which together comprise a subordinate stratum of a large, hierarchically-arranged state.

Despite the great diversity among peasant peoples, many anthropologists believe that certain generalizations about them hold true in most national settings. Foster (1962:45) writes that there are marked similarities in peasant life around the world, and Redfield (1956:25) believed that "peasant society and culture has something generic about it." Rogers (1969) surveyed many of the anthropological and sociological studies of peasants and concluded that the following ten elements are central components of a "subculture of peasantry": (1) mutual distrust in interpersonal relations; (2) perceived limited good; (3) dependence on and hostility toward government authority; (4) familism; (5) lack of innovativeness; (6) fatalism; (7) limited aspiration; (8) lack of deferred gratification; (9) limited view of the world; and (10) low empathy. Rogers rightly warns that exceptions to this broad generalization do exist, and in this study we will see some exceptions, especially to items seven and ten.

As impressive as the accomplishments of the various social scientists studying peasants have been, this broad area of research and theorizing is only in its adolescent stage. In his recent review of the subject, Frederick Gamst (1974:2) has judged that "much of the growth of the cultural anthropological theory of peasant culture and the bulk of the ethnographic data on it have been generated since 1960. Today's students of peasants may therefore be considered contemporary pioneers in social science."

NOTES

1. The full title of this work is *Hayriye Köy Araştırma ve Planlama Çalışması* [Hayriye Village Research and Planning Study].

2. By necessity, our discussion of the peasant concept is brief and elementary, being intended primarily for the general reader. For a much more complete treatment of the concept and its associated controversy, we refer you to Potter *et al.* (1967), Shanin (1971, 1973), Wolf (1966), and the various issues of the *Peasant Studies Newsletter*.

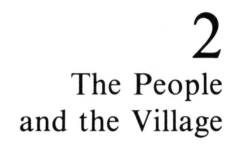

2
The People
and the Village

Because the Georgians are one of the world's most esoteric peoples whose past is nevertheless abundantly rich, we have chosen to devote the first part of this chapter to a brief discussion of their history and homeland. The chapter's second part describes their settlement in Turkey and the village of Hayriye.

The Caucasus and Its Peoples

The Caucasus region is the area of southeastern Europe occupying the isthmus between the Black and Caspian Seas. The region's most striking natural feature is the lofty Caucasus mountain range, stretching about 750 miles from the Black Sea's Taman Peninsula southeasterly to the Caspian's Apsheron Peninsula. Its highest peak is Mt. Elbrus (18,510 ft.; 5,642 m.).

This mountainous place was known to the ancient Greeks as *Kaukasos*, from which comes the Latin *Caucasus*, which speakers of other European languages subsequently adopted. The name is not of Caucasian origin, but may derive from the ancient Iranian *krou-kasis*, meaning "ice-covered" or "ice resplendent" (Menges 1956:19). In 1975 the German anthropolgist

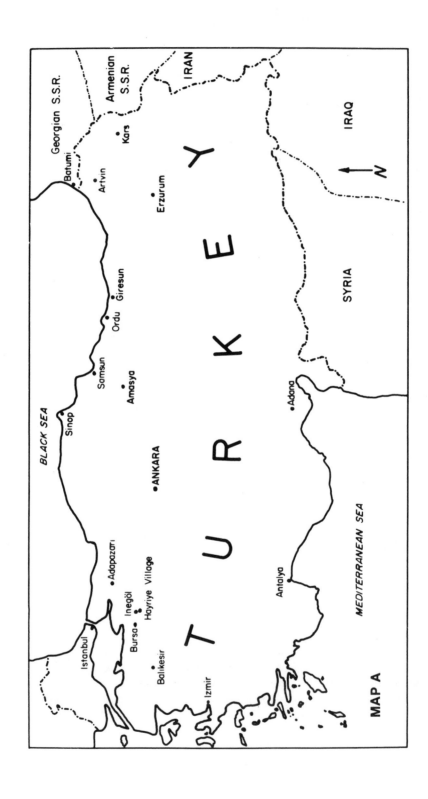

MAP A

Johann Blumenbach, believing erroneously that Caucasia was the home of the hypothetical Indo-Europeans, used the term Caucasian as a racial designation.

Today the region is occupied by several of the Soviet Union's political divisions: Armenian SSR, Georgia SSR, Azerbaijan SSR, Dagestan ASSR, Kabardinian ASSR, Chechen-Ingush ASSR, North Ossetian ASSR, and others. The Georgian Soviet Socialist Republic is nestled around the eastern tip of the Black Sea, just south of the great barrier formed by the Caucasus Mountains. With few exceptions, such as the fertile plain of Kolkhida—the site of ancient Colchis—the Georgian terrain is largely mountainous (85% of the total area), and a third is covered by forest and brushwood.

The Caucasus has been known for centuries as an ethnic mosaic, and currently over one-third of the nations and tribes of the entire USSR reside in this comparatively small region (Luzbetak 1951:1). Nowhere else are there so many different peoples found in such a small area. In the first century A.D. Strabo mentions that in the town of Dioskurias (Sukhume) on the Black Sea Coast, representatives of no less than 70 peoples, all speaking different languages, gathered to carry on trade. In the same century, Pliny the Elder writes that the Romans carried on their business in the Caucasus through eighty interpreters. The Arab geographers called the Caucasus "the mountain of languages" (Kuipers 1956a:377-78).

Caucasia's ethnic mosaic achieved its peculiar arrangement through the successive migrations and inextricable blending of many diverse peoples over numerous generations. The Caucasian valleys and mountain strongholds provided natural refuge for peoples moving south from the Eurasian plain or north from Asia Minor and the Iranian plateau. From ancient times to the present, great powers outside the Caucasus have played a dominant role in its history. The Sumerian, Hittite, Babylonian, and Assyrian empires of the ancient world extended their influence into the Caucasus along with Troy and the other Aegean civilizations. During the classical period, the Greeks and Romans vied with the Achaemenids of Persia and, later, the Parthians for control of the region. They were succeeded in this rivalry for Caucasian supremacy by the empires of the Byzantines, Sassanians, Khazars, Arabs, Ottomans, and finally the Russians.

For purposes of classification, this complex mosaic has been simplified somewhat by dividing the inhabitants into "indigenous" and extrageneous peoples on the basis of linguistic and historical evidence.[1] The indigenous peoples, referred to as the Paleo-caucasians, speak languages belonging to no other linguistic groups outside the Caucasus, while the "non-Caucasians" include speakers of languages belonging to external linguistic

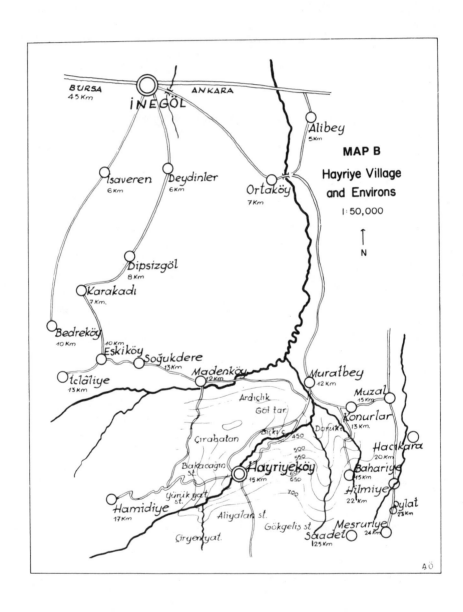

groups, such as Indo-European, Altaic, and Semitic. Among the "non-Caucasians" are the Armenians, Russians and other Slavs, Kurds, Ossetes, Persians, Mongols, Turks, Arabs, and Jews.

Paleo-caucasians. On the basis of linguistic criteria the Paleo-caucasians have been divided into three groups: a Southern group of about 2,250,000 people, a Northwestern group of about 350,000 people, and a Northeastern group of about 1,300,000 people (estimates from Kuipers 1956a:380).

The Northwestern Caucasians consist of the Abkhaz (*Ap'sua*)[2], the Circassians (*Adighe*), and the Ubykh (*P'yokh*). In 1865 the entire Ubykh population emigrated to Turkey to avoid Russian domination.

The Northeastern Caucasians exhibit the greatest linguistic diversity and constitute six linguistic branches: a) Veinakh; b) Avaro-Ando-Dido; c) Lak-Dargwa; d) Samurian; e) Khinalug; and f) Udi. Speakers of languages comprising the first four linguistic branches are often referred to collectively as "Lezgians."

The Southern Caucasians consist of the Mingrelians (*Megreli*); the Laz (*Tsani*) (most of whom live in Turkey); the Svans; and the Georgians (*Kartvelni*).

The Georgians, who number over 2,000,000 in the USSR and over 60,000 in Turkey, are the most numerous of the Paleocaucasian peoples and have the oldest political tradition and an alphabet dating back to the 5th century A.D. They call themselves *Kartveli* (pl., *Kartvelni*) and their homeland *Sakartvelo*. The European designations for them, e.g., Italian *Georgiano*, French *Georgien*, and English Georgian, derive from the Persian *Gurdj* (pl., *Gurdjan*), which was altered by the European Crusaders to resemble the name of Saint George (Kuipers 1956a:381).

The Georgians are divided into two dialect groups by the Surami Mountains. The Eastern Group is comprised of Kartli, Kakheti, Ingilo, Tush, Khevsur, Pshavs, Mokhev, and Mtiul, and the Western group consists of Imereti, Racha, and Guria. The Georgian Adcharians (Adzhars), who live in the Batumi area, speak the same dialect as the Gurians, their northern neighbors, but differ from them culturally by being Muslims (Kuipers 1956a:380-82). The Muslim Georgian settlers of Hayriye village were Adcharians.

The Georgians. In all probability the Georgians are not autochthonous to the Caucasus (Halasi-Kun 1956:268). They may result from the fusion of aboriginal inhabitants with immigrants who entered the Caucasus from Asia Minor in remote antiquity (Lang 1962:18). The ancestors of the Georgian nation appear early in the 1st millenium B.C. in the annals of Assyria and, later, of Urartu (in today's Armenia). Two of the tribal names mentioned are the Diauhi and the Kulkha, ancestors of the Colchians, who controlled large territories at the eastern end of the Black Sea. The fabled

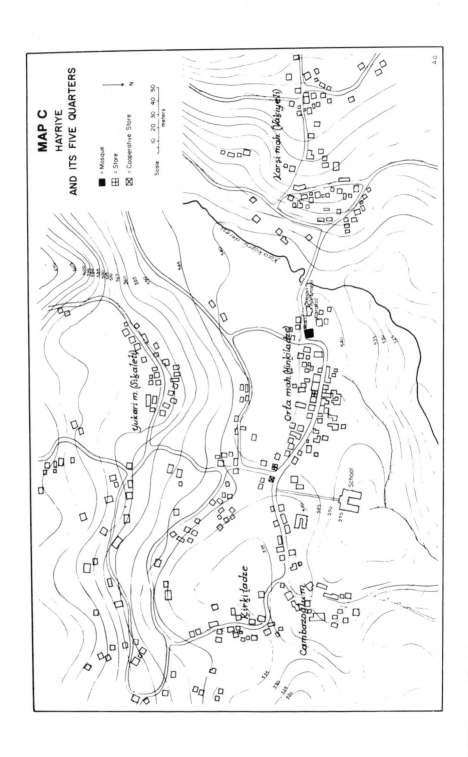

wealth of Colchis (Western Georgia) was known to the Greeks and found expression in the legend of Medea and the Golden Fleece.

Greek settlers from Miletus colonized Colchis from 600 B.C. onward. During the fifth century B.C. the Georgians fell under the hegemony of the Persian Achaemenid Empire of Cyrus the Great and Darius. After the campaigns of Alexander the Great in the 4th century B.C., the Georgians established the Kingdom of Iberia east of Colchis.

By 65 B.C. Pompey's Roman legions had forced the Georgians into dependent status. According to the geographer Strabo, the Romans found Iberia a rich land with two ecological zones—the mountainous uplands and the river valleys. The more populous highlanders engaged in animal husbandry and formed the mainstay of the armed forces; the lowlanders primarily cultivated gardens, orchards, and vineyards. Iberian society, Strabo wrote, was stratified into four main classes: the royal family and priests making up the first and second; free farmers, herdsmen, and warriors comprising the third; and serf laborers, domestic slaves, and prisoners of war forming the fourth. Strabo does not mention a Georgian merchant and artisan class, possibly because it was composed of Jews, Greeks, Persians, Syrians, and other non-Georgians (Lang 1962:24-25).

With Roman officials and legionaries stationed at strategic points along the Black Sea and in garrisons in the interior, Georgian sociocultural life came under new, strong influences. The Romans built roads which gave the country access to markets in other parts of the Roman Empire and accelerated the spread of new customs, products, and techniques throughout the land. During the 3rd century A.D. Roman power declined and the Sassanids of Iran gained political supremacy over Eastern Georgia, thereby exposing it to Persian culture and Zoroastrian religion.

By the 3rd century a new ideology—Christianity—had entered the Caucasus. Neighboring Armenia embraced the religion first, and thereby became the oldest Christian state on earth. Georgia's conversion to Christianity followed. According to tradition, a captive holy woman from Cappadocia, later known as St. Nino, inspired the conversion in 337 A.D., during the reign of Constantine the Great. Christianity provided the Georgians with a cohesive force which withstood the divisive pressures created by the successive invasions and counter-invasions of the great powers that vied for political control over the Caucasus.

During the next six centuries the Byzantine and Iranian Empires controlled different parts of Georgia. The Arab caliphs entered the scene during the 7th century and established an amirate in Tbilisi (Tiflis) in 654 A.D. Georgian national independence began to rise during the 11th century and reached its zenith in the next century under the reign (1184-

1213) of Queen Tamara, whose realm encompassed a pan-Caucasian empire with borders extending north to south from Cherkessia to Azerbaijan and east to west from Gandzha (Kirovabad) to Erzurum. Although the Queen ruled by the doctrine of divine right, her powers were checked by the existence of strong feudal institutions (Lang 1962:29).

Georgia's golden age was terminated by the Mongol invasions occurring from 1220 onward, and Eastern Georgia was reduced to vassalage under the Mongol Il Khans of Hulagu's line. A flicker of national independence ignited during the reign (1314-46) of Georgia's King Giorgi V, but it was quickly extinguished by the onslaughts of Timur (Tamerlane, a descendant of Genghiz Khan) between 1386 and 1403.

These events were followed by further Georgian misfortunes. The Ottoman Turks' conquest of Byzantium and capture of Constantinople in 1453 isolated Georgia from western Christendom. The Ottomans temporarily assumed the Byzantines' former sphere of influence. During the next several centuries the Ottomans, who were Sunni ("Orthodox") Muslims, and the various Iranian dynasties, which were Shiite ("Heterodox") Muslims, continued the incessant rivalry for dominance in the Caucasus. For much of this period the Ottomans controlled the western Caucasus and propagated Sunni Islam among the Georgian and Circassian mountain tribes. Most likely, it was during the 16th or 17th century that the Gurian-Adcharian ancestors of the settlers of Hayriye village converted to Sunni Islam and developed a close cultural relationship with the Ottoman Turks.

In the 16th century, a third force, Russia, entered the Caucasian battle scene from the north and posed a threat to the Ottomans. The Christian princes of Georgia began to look upon Christian Russia as a protector against the Muslim invaders from the west and south. Eventually, however, the Russian protector became master.

Over the next several centuries the Russians engaged the Turks all along their common borders, from the Balkans to the Caucasus, and wrested extensive territories from the faltering Ottomans. During the Russo-Turkish War of 1877-78, when the main Russian and Turkish forces were locked in their usual massive combat on the Balkan front, the Russians made great advances in western Caucasia and eastern Anatolia. Following the war, the Congress of Berlin confirmed Russia's possession of Adchara-Kobuleti, Artvin, Kars, and Ardahan—territories which had belonged to the medieval Georgian kingdom before their capture by the Ottomans. It was then that the Georgian settlers of Hayriye and many other Muslim Georgians fled to western Turkey, preferring Ottoman sovereignty to that of Russia. They joined the thousands of Muslim Circassians who had

FIG. 1

HAYRIYE POPULATION
BY AGE AND SEX
1962

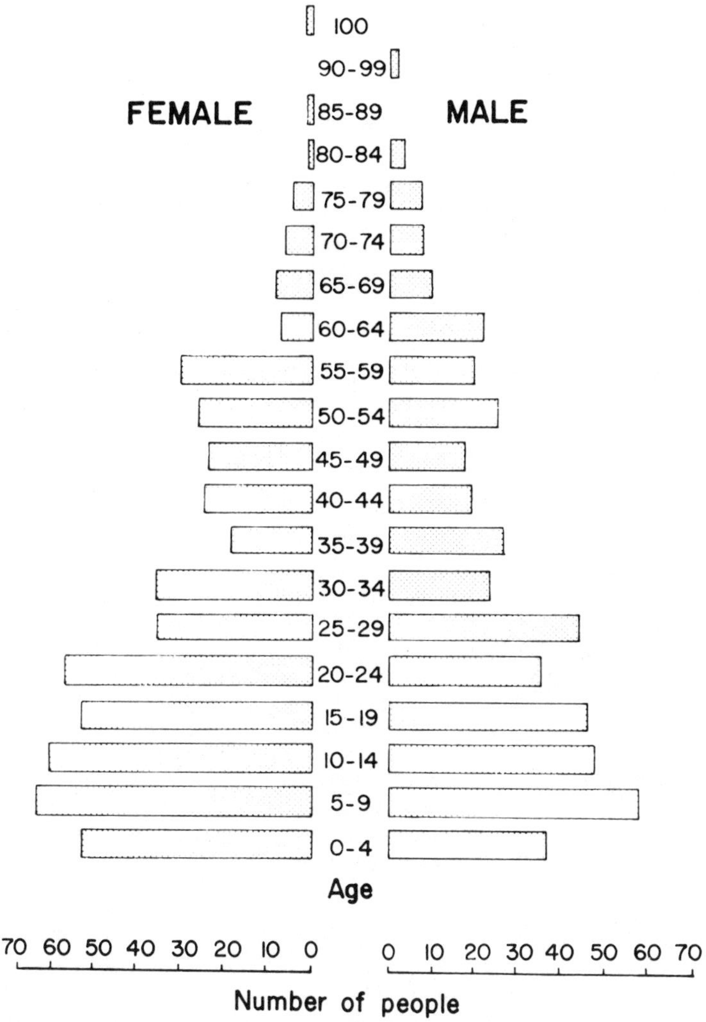

escaped to Turkey in 1864 after the Russians defeated their leader Sheik Shamil.

Many of the Muslim Georgians who remained behind met their doom during World War I, when the Caucasus again proved to be an important secondary battlefield. In April 1915 Turkish units supported by Muslim Georgian Laz and Adchar irregulars attempted to raid the Russian-held Black Sea port of Batumi, but were repulsed. In retaliation, the Russian General Lyakhov was sent to slaughter the Georgian Laz and Adchars for their pro-Turkish attitude. "Lyakhov ravaged and depopulated the entire Chorokhi valley up to Artvin, in the vicinity of which only 7,000 out of a previous population of 52,000 Georgian Muslims were left alive" (Lang 1962:185).

At the end of the war, Kemalist Turkey was ceded most of the Anatolian land Russia had taken from the Ottomans in 1877-78. Kars, Artvin, and Ardahan went to Turkey, while Batumi and the surrounding region of Adchara were retained by the Soviet Union. Georgia was incorporated into the Soviet Union in 1921 as part of the Transcaucasian Soviet Federated Socialist Republic. In 1936 this federation was dissolved and Georgia became a Soviet Socialist Republic in its own right.

Historian D.M. Lang has offered some depictions of Georgian national character which we find interesting. We include them here with the proviso that they, like all such characterizations, be regarded with caution. He begins by quoting Prince Vakhushti's 18th century description of his fellow-countrymen (Lang 1962:18):

> 'In outward appearance, the men and women are comely and handsome, black of eye, brow and hair; their complexion is white and rosy, less frequently swarthy or sallow .... They are slim of waist, the girls particularly, and seldom stout; they are brave and hard-working, with great powers of endurance, bold cavaliers and eager for a fray, nimble and quick off the mark .... They are doughty warriors, lovers of arms, haughty, audacious; and so avid of personal glory that they will sacrifice their fatherland or their sovereign for the sake of their own advancement; they are hospitable to guests and strangers, and cheerful of disposition; if two or three are assembled together, they are never at a loss for amusement; they are generous and prodigal of their own goods and of other people's, and never think of amassing possessions; they are intelligent, quick-witted, self-centered and lovers of learning .... They lend loyal support to one another and will remember and repay a good turn but will exact retribution for an insult. They change rapidly from a good mood to a bad one; are headstrong, ambitious, and apt both to flatter and to take offence ....'

Next, Lang himself writes as follows (1962:18-19).

> Georgian women share with those of Circassia a high reputation for grace and beauty, and in olden times were often carried off to grace the

harems of the Ottoman Sultans and the Shahs of Persia. The Georgians are not an inhibited race, though they preserve a rigid code of sexual morality. They produce excellent wine and are lavish with hospitality. A French traveller entering Georgia from Turkey in 1701 expressed himself delighted with his reception at the hands of the honest country folk, who 'come and present you with all manner of provisions, bread, wine, fowls, hogs, lambs, sheep'. He contrasted the Georgians' smiling and courteous manners with the 'serious fellows that survey you gravely from head to foot' in Turkey....

The Georgians have always been renowned as men-at-arms. In Roman times, Pompey found the Iberians hard to vanquish; their king, Artag, and his spirited followers, defeated in pitched battle, climbed up trees and shot at the Roman legions until the forests themselves were chopped or burnt down....The mediaeval Arabic writer al-'Umari, who served the Mamluk Sultan of Egypt, described Georgia as 'an extensive land and an important kingdom', whose warriors were 'the kernel of the religion of the Cross and a people of courage and valour'.

Finally the historian warns against idealizing the Georgian character (Lang 1962:20):

Every medal has its reverse. In many Georgians, quick wit is matched by a quick temper, and a proneness to harbour rancour. The bravery associated with heroes like Prince Bagration, an outstanding general of the Napoleonic wars, is matched by the cruelty and vindictiveness found in such individuals as Stalin and Beri.

The Village of Hayriye

Fearing potential Russian persecution at the end of the Russo-Turkish War of 1877-78, thousands of Muslim Georgians fled their Caucasian homeland and sailed from Batumi to Giresun, Ordu, Samsun, Sinop, Istanbul, and other Turkish ports. Some remained near these port cities; others traveled inland and settled villages in the provinces of Amasya, Adapazarı, Bursa, and Balıkesir.

About 250 of these Georgian immigrants left their village near Artvin, which today is on the Turkish side of the Turco-Georgian border, and traveled to the province of Bursa. According to today's villagers, their forefathers were led to the site of Hayriye by Haci Mehmet Efendi, a Georgian *imam* ("Muslim prayer leader"), who was living in the nearby Turkish village of Maden. On an earlier trip to this site the *imam* had been struck by the close similarity between the weather, forests, and river valleys of this hilly place and the natural features of his native Georgia. Consequently, he claimed the spot for a group of his fellow countrymen.

Once the Georgian settlers arrived, however, they found that a group of Circassian immigrants had already taken possession of the site and were sheltering in the hollows of large plane trees. An argument between the two peoples over their conflicting territorial claims led to fighting and a Circassian retreat. To resolve the issue, the two sides later argued their cases peacefully before the district governor in Inegöl. He decided to let the Georgians occupy the controversial spot and directed the Circassians to another site, now called Hacikara village. Reportedly, during his deliberation, the governor repeatedly expressed his hope that good (Turk. "*hayır*") would come from his decision. For this reason, the Georgians contend, their village was designated Hayriye. (Hayriye is a derivation of *hayır*.)

The Georgian immigrants spent the first winter as guests of Turkish villagers in Maden. Come spring, individual households staked their claims to home sites and land. It is said that because land was abundant, no disputes arose, even though shares were not equal. Georgian *ağa*s—the heads of wealthy households—were able to claim and develop more land than the others because of their numerically superior human and animal resources. Consequently, previous socioeconomic status differences were preserved.

Villagers from Maden and nearby Ortaköy helped the Georgians cut timber, build their homes and barns, and clear fields for planting. The Georgians received no material aid from the Ottoman government, until 1895 when they constructed their small village mosque.

With a high natural birth rate and added Georgian immigration (including a few Laz families) Hayriye quickly grew in size and importance. During the Turkish War of Independence (1919-1923) the district's gendarmery station was placed in the village. Later, the district forestry office was also located there, and for a few years, the village was elevated to the rank of *nahiye* ("district seat"). Interestingly, these governmental agencies were not placed in Hayriye because of its centrality to other villages in the administrative district. On the contrary, Hayriye is one of the most remote and inaccessible of villages. The agencies were located there primarily because of Hayriye's proximity to an important source of government revenue—the mountain forest—which officials want to protect from villagers seeking fuel and building materials.

The vast majority of Hayriye's inhabitants have been immigrant Georgians. The most numerically significant exceptions being a few immigrant Laz families and several households of formerly nomadic Turks—Yürüks—who were residing in the area when the Georgians arrived. They belonged to the Sheyit tribe, most of whose members now live in Kutahya Province. Reportedly, these Yürüks had been grazing their flocks on the hill pastures near the site of Hayriye for generations. Their present-day descendants claim their ancestors could have secured a title deed to the village site if they had bribed certain Ottoman officials. This they refused to do, and subsequently the Georgians got the land. The Yürüks stayed on, however, and lived harmoniously with the newcomers.

As Table 1 demonstrates, over the years the village's population climbed to an upper limit of just above 1,000 and then dropped off after the 1965 census. The reason for this decrease—emigration to Europe—is the subject of later chapters.

Table 1
Hayriye Population Figures

Year:	1880	1940	1945	1950	1955	1965	1970	1974
Population	250	955	1026	1083	1063	1010	746	750

Source: Village records. The 1880 and 1974 figures are estimates.

Villages in this area are distinctly separate from each other geographically, and their dwellings tend to be centrally clustered. As in other parts of the Middle East, each village constitutes a clearly defined ecological and psychosocial entity with definite borders (cf. Tannous 1942). Homes scattered between villages are rarely seen.

The Turkish Ministry of Interior classifies Hayriye as a "mountain village," as it is located in the foothills of the Uludağ range. The settlement's general terrain is splintered by ravines and gorges, and its northern edge is more recently being eaten away by erosion. Its mountain soil is less fertile than that of villages on the alluvial plain.

The village was originally settled in a roughly linear fashion along a dirt road that marked an east-west axis. In time, it expanded south and farther west, encroaching on the forested mountain slopes. The village is comprised of five residential quarters, each containing a cluster of 30 to 40 homes and their outbuildings (see Map C). Tree groves, gardens, small grazing areas, a river, and a stream separate the quarters from each other. The roads connecting the quarters are a mixture of stone and a dirt that turns to dust in summer and mud in winter. An aerial view of Hayriye reveals that its dominant colors are the red of its tiled roofs and the green of its trees, gardens, and fields. (A description of homesteads and outbuildings appears in Chapter V.)

Central Quarter, which in Turkish is called *Orta* and in Georgian *Hinkiladze*—the name of a dominant lineage, contains the village's mosque, primary schools, coffeehouses, general stores, and government offices (see Map C). It provides the locus for most public activities. Two other quarters, which are referred to exclusively by lineage names—

Cambazoğlu and Kirkitadze—lie to its east. Upper Quarter (Turk. *Yukarı*; Georg. *Sikaleti*) lies to the south, and Opposite Quarter (Turk. *Karşı*; Georg. *Vakiyeli*) are to the west. Uninhabited spaces between the edges of Central Quarter and the other four quarters do not exceed 60 meters in length. Central and Cambazoğlu quarters sit at about 540 m. above sea level; the others climb to an elevation of 600 m.

The residential part of the village is bounded on the north and east by cultivated fields and on the south and west by mountain slopes covered with forests of chestnut, beech, pine, and oak. Several gentle slopes in the higher elevations are used as alpine pastures, where village livestock can graze on green grass during the height of summer.

Geology. Hayriye village is nestled in hills approximately 15 kilometers south of the city of Inegöl. The first nine–kilometer stretch of land from Inegol to the village consists mostly of an alluvial flood plain in which clay and silty materials predominate. Neogene continental deposits crop out in the remaining six kilometers. The contact between the two is easily recognized due to differences in their topographic expression. The recent alluvial surface is generally smooth, whereas the older, eroded Neogene strata are markedly irregular and hilly. Most of the Neogene deposits consist of shales and poorly consolidated sandstones. Surface erosion of this material has produced slumping and landslides. Periodic flood waters from the area's rivers and streams have washed away much of the top soil, greatly reducing the land's fertility. The soil is moist to a depth of one to 1.5 meters; the water table occurs at 5 meters, and bedrock at 7 meters (*Hayriye Köy Araştırma* pp. 19-20).

Geologist Van der Kaaden, who investigated the area in 1952, described the Neogene and Paleozoic contact in the south of Hayriye village as a fault. However, Turkish geologists, who examined the region in the early 1960s, contradict this conclusion, claiming that it is a normal depositional contact. The geologists do agree that the area contains no economically exploitable minerals (ibid).

Climate. Hayriye's weather is temperate, with warm days and cool nights in summer and a mild cold in winter. The following weather information comes from the village's closest meteorologic station in Inegöl, about 15 kilometers to the north. Because Inegöl's average elevation is 310 meters as compared to 550 meters for Hayriye, its weather conditions vary somewhat from those of the village. In general, Inegöl is warmer.

During a two-year observational period, Inegöl's average annual temperature of 12.3° C. ranged from an average low of .8° C. in January to an average high of 22.2° C. in July. The lowest and highest temperatures recorded in a six-year observational period were -21.2° C. in February and 41.5° C. in August. Relative humidity varies from an average high of 78% in February to an average low of 58% in July. Percipitation, averaging 501.3 mm. annually, occurs mostly in winter, with the highest amounts in December, January, and March (averaging about 62 mm. each) and the lowest in August (6.5 mm. ave.). Snow falls about five days a year. Cool, northwesterly breezes prevail in the summer and give way to mild, southwesterly *lodos* winds the rest of the year (*Bursa II Yıllığı / 1967*).

NOTES

1. Aside from the articles by Catford (1977) and Gamkrelidze and Gudava (1974), linguists have written little in English which describes the various Caucasian languages. According to Catford, the best general introduction to the subject is the fourth volume of the Russian series *Jazyki narodov SSR* (Languages of the Peoples of the USSR) (Moscow: Nauka, 1967).

2. These peoples' designations for themselves appear in parentheses.

Fig. 2 A village *bagen*

Fig. 3 Hayriye boys with toy "cars"

3
Village Kinship
and Social Organization

In Hayriye, village households owning sufficient land and animals may approach economic self-sufficiency, but they cannot survive as social isolates. To some extent, they must rely on other households and in turn be relied on for mutual social, economic, political, and spiritual support. Because the village's basic resources—land, water, pasturage, and manpower—exist in limited supply, village stability, harmony, and ultimate survival depend on the achievement of at least three prerequisites: a general recognition of rights and obligations with respect to resources and people; a system of sanctions to support social norms; and a degree of cooperation and mutual aid among residents. Here, as in many societies, kinship represents a system of social integration which intimately links groups of people for the purpose of achieving these ends.

In the following description of kinship and social organization in Hayriye, we occasionally refer to Georgian practices in the Caucasus, but we do not offer a comparison between pre- and post-migration customs. We hope that those who are interested in conducting such a comparative study will find our material on Hayriye of some use.

Kinship Units, Inheritance, and Descent

Even prior to the Georgians' immigration to Turkey, their kinship system resembled that of the Turks (Luzbetak 1951). The similarities between the two systems of kinship stem partly from the fact that for centuries these peoples lived in close contact with each other, sharing the same Islamic faith and nearly identical modes of ecological adaptation.

Since their immigration to Turkey, the Georgians of Hayriye have conformed even more to Turkish kinship and social practices. For example, certain Turkish kinship terms, such as *baba* ("father"), *hala* ("mother's sister"), *gelin* ("son's wife", "new bride"), *yenge* ("father's brother's wife"), and *badızı* ("wife's sister"), have replaced their Georgian equivalents in ordinary conversation. In addition, these Georgians use the same terms as the Turks for several basic kinship units and spiritual kinship ties (see below) and now condone marriages between second cousins which they formerly prohibited.

Like the Georgians of the Caucasus and the Turks of Anatolia, the people of Hayriye trace descent through males primarily and pass most property, particularly homes, out-buildings, land, and animals, through the patriline. Although the paternal estate can be alienated, village custom grants a son exclusive right to repurchase his paternal home for its original selling price plus a consideration for major improvements, despite the passage of years and the growth of inflation.

This right had been exercised by a Georgian male I interviewed. The man had been born in Hayriye, but left the village during his youth. He became a career military officer and eventually settled in Ankara, Turkey's capital. Meanwhile, his father sold the family's village home and moved to Inegöl, where he retired and then died. Years passed, and the son began visiting his friends and remaining relatives in Hayriye during summer vacations. During one of these visits he reminisced with friends about his boyhood home and wished aloud that his father had not sold it. The villagers then informed him of his right as a son to reclaim his paternal home from its present owner. So he went to the owner, who recognized his right and sold him the house for only TL 300, the purchase price of about two decades previous.

Daughters commonly receive a portion of the paternal wealth in the form of trousseau items prior to marriage. In addition, young girls of the more well-to-do families customarily are given garden plots in which they cultivate vegetables for their fathers' households. When and if they marry men in the village, they receive full ownership of these gardens in which they can henceforth produce food for their own husbands and children. Daughters marrying outside the village, however, generally lose claim to the gardens, which remain part of the paternal estate.

It appears that in the past, especially, most villagers regarded the patrilocal extended household as the ideal domestic unit under typical circumstances.[1] In an agrarian village, where land is limited and non-farming occupations are few, most young men who remain in the village are economically dependent on their fathers, and most fathers need their sons' labor. Under these conditions, the patrilocal extended household, which functions both as a unit of production and consumption, represents a highly adaptive structure for organizing labor and supporting new families. Commonly, a newly married man, not employed outside the village, remains in his father's home for at least a few years. If he can achieve economic independence, he usually separates and establishes his own household. Otherwise, he may stay until the patriarch's death.[2]

According to the METU study conducted in 1961-62, Hayriye household sizes ranged from two to twelve persons, with the average being 5.11 (*Hayriye Köy Araştırma* 1963:14,89). No one was living alone. The study found that household size varied directly with economic status: the richest households were the largest, the poorest the smallest. Every year the village chief and council of elders rank all households on the basis of their wealth into seven categories for purposes of village tax (*salma*) assessment. Households ranked first pay the maximum (TL 20; about $2.22), those ranked seventh pay the minimum (TL 2). Households ranked from second to sixth pay TL 16, TL 12.50, TL 9, TL 7, and TL 4 respectively.[3] The numbers, average sizes, and total populations of Hayriye households are cross-tabulated by economic rank in Table 2. The table evinces the importance of a viable economic foundation for the maintenance of large, extended households.[4]

Table 2
Hayriye Household Sizes by Economic Rank
1961

Economic Rank	No. of Households	Ave. Size	Population
1	8	9.00	72
2	9	7.11	64
3	30	6.17	185
4	47	5.32	250
5	51	4.59	234
6	27	3.19	86
7	6	3.17	19
Totals	178		910

Source: *Hayriye Köy Araştırma* 1963:14

The METU researchers also conducted interviews in a representative sample of 10% of Hayriye households and found that 47.6% of them consisted of only one nuclear family each, while 29.4% were formed by patrilocal extended families. The remaining 23% also consisted of extended families (usually a nuclear family plus the dependent father or mother of the husband), but had not been formed by the ideal patrilocal process. In these cases the sons did not bring their new wives into their parents' homes, but rather the parents joined their sons' families as dependents (*Hayriye Köy Araştırma* 1963:89).

Many patrilocal extended households are of the stem type, consisting of a patriarch, matriarch, and only one married son (usually the oldest) and his wife and children. Because of the limited productive capacity of the lands owned by these households, younger sons had to leave and find independent livelihoods. In many cases, the sons immigrated to Inegöl or other Turkish cities; more recently, many have gone to Europe. Over the years, a few Hayriye households have been joint fraternal ones, composed of two brothers and their families. They resulted from originally patrilocal extended households that suffered the death of their patriarchs. In these few cases, the brothers and their families got on well and decided to remain together jointly working the paternal estate. Normally, however, married brothers living in a patrilocal extended household will separate when their father dies.

Hayriye's 1961 average household size of 5.11 persons is not typical of villages in Turkey. According to the 1965 Turkish census average household sizes for all of Turkey were 6.16 persons for villages, 5.22 for towns, and 4.69 for cities (*Genel Nüfus Sayımı* 1965:673-75). And in a 1968 village survey, the average household size was 6.6 for a nationwide, representative sample of 220 villages, and 6.3 for a Marmara region sub-sample (*Modernization in Turkish Villages* 1974: 163,187). The comparatively small figure for Hayriye is largely attributable to a steady immigration to cities since the thirties.

A household's internal organization is largely determined by its composition, the personalities of its members, and idealized role expectations. In most households the eldest male is the patriarch— an authority figure who demands respect and obedience from all females and younger males. His wife, the matriarch, is also respected, but her relationships with her offspring and their children are warm and affectionate. Although the patriarch commands supreme authority in theory, in actuality the household is mother-centered. The mother, being mostly confined to the home and its immediate neighborhood, manages and directs its internal affairs.[5] The traditional division of labor assigns women responsibility for the internal home and men the duty of providing most of the household's food and income, as well as representing it in the external world. A husband has responsibility for his wife's actions, but should not interfere with her domestic work. In public and before visitors, the wife is expected to act submissively, devotedly, and respectfully to her husband. In private, a strong-willed woman can dominate a weaker man. Sexual fidelity is expected of both spouses, but public displays of mutual affection are not condoned.

Male and female behavior in general is largely circumscribed by social norms designed to preserve family honor and avoid shame. In Hayriye, as in Turkey and throughout much of the Mediterranean world, critical points of honor rest on a man's relationship to his women, especially his mother, sisters, wife, and daughters (cf. Peristiany 1966). If his women maintain their purity in traditional cultural terms, he keeps his honor. Should they become tainted, his honor turns to shame. The preservation of female purity has traditionally required seclusion from unrelated men. Exposure may encourage flirting or other sexual suggestions which are sufficient to defile a woman and dishonor her men. Men regain their honor by punishing the woman, if she facilitated the shame, and by gaining revenge on the persons who defiled her. Hence, defilement may lead to serious conflict within and between families. To reduce the chances of such situations occurring, unrelated men and women should practice mutual avoidance. Furthermore, women should keep themselves fully covered, except for their hands and eyes, when in the view of unrelated men.[6]

Among household members women are free to expose their face, arms, and hair, but little more. Should the household contain more than one married couple, each sleeps with their young children in a separate room, although the entire household—men, women, and children—eat together around a slightly raised tray which holds common bowls of food.

Probably the most intimate social ties in a household are those among mothers, daughters, and sisters. A young girl normally spends her entire pre-marital life in close association with her mother and sisters, sharing chores and learning domestic arts. They become true confidants and friends. But as close as the mother-daughter relationship is, every woman regards the birth of a son as a special gift from Allah.[7] A son increases her status in the eyes of her husband, her in-laws, and the entire community. Hence, she pampers and attends him closely throughout his youth. He remains close to her until puberty; then he begins to identify more closely with men and to spend most of his free time with male peers.

The father-daughter relationship begins tenderly, but progressively formalizes. While an older daughter may argue and joke with her mother, she commonly relates to her father with quiet obedience and deference. The two rarely display mutual affection in public, especially after the daughter reaches puberty.

Relations between father and son are at once complex, delicate, and critical to a household's stability. The idealized Georgian male adult is an independent-minded, self-determined person who willingly cooperates with his kin and neighbors for their mutual good, but who begrudges almost all authority over him. Hence, a father's demand for his son's complete respect and obedience often produces tension and can easily lead to open conflict. Yet, a father and son are often economically interdependent (the father owns the land, but needs his son's labor) and cooperation between them is essential for the well-being of the household. When the two are together in public or with an outsider, the son must observe numerous rules of formal decorum. If the father stands, the son should not sit. If the father sits in a chair, the son should either stand, squat, or sit on the floor. The son should talk as little and as respectfully as possible. He should neither smoke, play cards, joke, nor do anything else that might be interpreted as casual behavior. In such situations the father, too, must act with more formal reserve than he might if his son were not present.

In order to reduce the number of these formal, tense situations in which a breach of decorum inevitably leads to reprimand and conflict, Georgian society has instituted avoidance rules for fathers and sons to observe in public places. For example, should a son see his father with a gathering of men, the son should avoid the group unless told to join it. And because all senior men are ideally entitled to the formal deference of their juniors, the rules of avoidance are extended. For instance, when a group of young men decide to go drink tea and talk, they will cautiously look into each of the village's two coffeehouses before entering to be sure their fathers or uncles are not there. If at all possible, they will choose the coffeehouse in which no senior men are present. If that is impossible, they will sit as far away from senior males as they can. Likewise, older men will avoid a coffeehouse in which their sons, nephews, or other junior males are already sitting.

During pre-pubescence, siblings of both sexes spend a great deal of time together in or near their home in a free and easy relationship. As they grow older, their statuses change, with the older sibling taking on many of the role characteristics of a parent of the corresponding sex vis-à-vis the younger. For example, an older sister becomes like a second mother to her younger siblings as she helps and guides them in a warm, patient, and understanding manner. Similarly, an older brother becomes like a second father by assuming the guardianship of family honor and a degree of authority over younger family members. After passing puberty, brothers and sisters should not display mutual affection in public, and brothers of disparate ages (four or more years difference) commonly observe the same public avoidance rules pertaining to fathers and sons.

Relations with kin outside the family follow the general pattern of internal relations. For example, the father's brother is considered "half a father" and, like the father, is an authority figure. While all older kin are treated with deference, kin on the father's side generally demand more formal respect than kin on the mother's side.

After the family and household the next largest kinship unit is the patrilineage, which the villagers term *gvari* in Georgian and *sülale* in Turkish. It is a noncorporate group of male and female members who trace descent through males to a common ancestor, but own no property rights in common. Beyond the household, patrilineage members represent primary sources of mutual aid and obligations, especially during times of crisis. Vertically, most villagers cannot trace their patrilineages beyond their own great-grandfathers; horizontally, every mature person knows all the living members of his patrilineage, even though they may exceed sixty people. Most patrilineage members have traditionally been neighbors as well as kin, since they have tended to reside in the same quarter.

According to Kuipers (1956b:528), in the Caucasus the Georgian "Pshav tribe (*dziri*, lit. "root") is divided into eleven clans (*temi*); the members of each clan bear the same name, but in everyday life are known under a second family name (*gvari*) derived from the proper name of a grandfather or great-grandfather. If a family expanded, new surnames were adopted." There are no clans in Hayriye, but Ahmet Ozkan recorded 43 patrilineage or *gvari* names there in the late 1950s. Some names, such as Dzvelaşvili (descendants of Dzvel), were completely Georgian; others, such as Alibegişvili (descendants of Alibeg), had Turkish or Arabic proper names with Georgian suffixes; and a few, like Bayraktaroğlu (sons of Bayraktar), were completely Turkish. The average number of families belonging to each patrilineage was four, while the range was from one to twelve. The village composition of some patrilineages had been reduced by emigration.

Although patrilineal names are regularly used in the village, they are not official names. During the Ottoman and early Republican period, the use of surnames in Turkey was not as common as it was in Europe, and many of the surnames in use were of Arabic, Persian, Caucasian, or other non-Turkic origin. In an effort to Turkify surnames and regularize their use, the Western-orientated government of reformist Kemal Ataturk passed a surname law, which became effective on January 1, 1935. Citizens were required to drop their non-Turkic surnames, if they had any, and register purely Turkish ones with designated government officials. Those without Turkish surnames could choose from a list specially drawn up for the occasion.

Consequently, most household heads in Hayriye were not able to register their patrilineal or *gvari* names as surnames. Some were able to Turkify their *gvari* names; for instance, Heyrisvili became Hayroğlu. Others chose completely different names; for example, household heads of the Goradze lineage chose Ceyhan, the name of a river in Turkey. In many cases, household heads of a single large lineage chose different names, thereby segmenting their lineage similarly to the way described by Kuipers (see above) for the Georgian Pshav tribe of the Caucasus. For example, the five household heads of the Kokoladze lineage chose five different surnames—Başyiğit, Bali, Turan, Varol, and Gurses—none of which resembles their original lineage name. Although present-day villagers still recognize *gvari* membership on the basis of their pre-1935 lineage names, in future decades their descendants will most likely narrow their range of recognition to those sharing the same legal surnames.

Marriage

According to Luzbetak (1951), the Georgians of the Caucasus practiced clan exogamy. That is, they prohibited marriage between persons of the same patrilineage and between persons of the different patrilineages forming the same clan. In Hayriye, the exogamous rule is not confined to kin on the father's side. In addition to the patrilineal prohibition, one should not marry any bilateral first cousin, the offspring of persons who have ritual kinship ties with one's parents, or an intimate neighbor, since children who grow up together are regarded almost as siblings. Furthermore, children who have suckled milk from the same woman, whoever she may be, are regarded as "milk siblings" and may not marry each other. Villagers say it is generally best to marry non-kin. They insist that first cousin marriages do not occur, but apparently under the influence of Turkish culture, there have been some second cousin marriages.

Even though Islam allows a man meeting certain conditions to have as many as four wives simultaneously, informants claim that multiple marriages traditionally have been uncommon in Hayriye. They could cite no more than two or three cases of bigamy existing at any one time. All informants—male and female—that I interviewed asserted that monogamy was the ideal. The Swiss Civil Code, adopted by Turkey in 1926, prohibits polygamy, but remained largely ineffectual for several decades. More recently, however, its application and increasing public acceptance have made it a real obstacle to multiple marriages in rural areas (see Magnarella 1973, 1974).

Because marriages involve interfamilial alliances and the acquisition of new relatives for both sides, they have traditionally been arranged by parents. Rural Turkish and Georgian culture prohibit courtship, but young people do meet secretly and fall in love. The young usually can express their marital preferences to their parents, and many do marry the person of their choice.[8] Strong-willed youths, who are denied this privilege, are apt to elope. One or two elopements occur annually in Hayriye, and if the rebellious youths have reached 18 years, the age of majority, there is little their offended parents can do but reluctantly accept the situation. Such couples have the legal right to marry. Furthermore, a girl who runs off with a boy ruins her reputation, so that no honorable family will knowingly accept her as a daughter-in-law. Hence, it is best for all concerned that she marry her lover and quietly settle down.

All parents want their offspring to marry someone from a "clean," honorable family that will not bring shame down upon them. The parents of a son prefer a daughter-in-law who will fit harmoniously into their household. She should be respectful and obedient, pretty, pleasant, and optimistic. Because Georgians in Hayriye practice hypergamy (women should marry men of equal or higher status than themselves), the parents of a daughter are especially concerned about their future son-in-law's finances. In addition, all parents, but especially daughters' parents, want their offspring to marry Georgians. Although Hayriye men occasionally marry non-Georgians, Hayriye women are reserved for Georgian men. "We take girls from others, but we do not give them."

Most males in recent years have married while in their early twenties or soon after completing compulsory military service. In the past they reportedly married somewhat younger. The trend for females, however, is reverse. Formerly, the average age was 18 or 19; recently it has been 15 or 16. Villagers reason that because girls are now freer and more exposed than before, parents want to marry them younger, before they get into sexual trouble and ruin their own and their families' reputations. Parents apparently want to marry their daughters while they are still in a position to choose spouses for them. Once daughters reach 18, they can legally marry without parental permission.

Because of the marital preferences and exogamous rules outlined above, most village marriages have tended to be inter-quarter unions between previously unrelated persons or distant relatives. Some Hayriye residents have married Georgians from other villages in the Inegöl Subprovince, and a few Hayriye men have married Circassians and Turkish women from villages nearby. Application of the hypergamous rule within a new context of social and economic development has resulted in a tendency for parents to marry their daughters to Georgian men well-situated in cities, and more recently Hayriye men successfully employed in Europe have become attractive spouses also.

As the above discussion indicates, Hayriye marriage practices function to widen each villager's network of kin. In addition to the relatives of one's own household and patrilineage, each villager also has a personal kindred.

Fig. 4   At the hearth

Fig. 5   Three generations

He or she shares a set of reciprocal rights and obligations for respect and support with a wide variety of kin to whom he is related either through his father (patrilaterally), mother (matrilaterally), or spouse (affinally). These kinship networks commonly extend throughout Hayriye, to nearby villages, to several Turkish cities (especially Inegöl, Bursa, and Istanbul), and even to Europe. Furthermore, these ties based on descent and marriage are complemented by institutionalized ritual kinship.

Ritual Kinship

Of the various ritual kinship practices in Hayriye, a form of co-parenthood called *kirvalık* locally produces the most comprehensive results. Unlike the Christian form of ritual coparenthood (*compadrazgo*) practiced in Latin America and Europe, *kirvalık* has no formal base in religious law. Neither *kirvalık* nor circumcision, with which it is associated, is mentioned in the *Quran*. It is known from pre-Islamic poetry, however, that the circumcision custom existed in early Arabia, and Muslim theologians trace its practice to Abraham (Gibb and Kramers 1953:254-55). The institution of *kirvalık* may also antedate Islam, and probably diffused to the Caucasus along with the spread of that faith. The word *kirva* (the reciprocal term used by the main parties to the ritual relationship) and its variants— *kirve, kiriv, kevra, kurva* —are not of Turkish derivation (see Koşay 1932; Dersimi 1952:32). The word may be indigenous to Kurdish and/or Farsi; in both languages the root *kirv* has the meaning of "penis" (Muin 1342 A.H.). The institution is found in a large region of the Middle East, including the Southern Caucasus, Northern Iraq, Northwestern Iran, and Eastern Turkey (Kırzıoğlu 1953: 504-505). It is not common in Western Turkey, except among peoples, such as Kurds and Georgians, who have emigrated from the East.[9]

Similar to *compadrazgo*, the Christian institution associated with baptism (Mintz and Wolf 1950), *kirvalık* involves three central elements: (1) a rite of passage—the circumcision of a male child, usually between the ages of seven and twelve; (2) a set of sociospiritual ties established between the participants; and (3) the sponsorship. The sponsor is almost always someone not already related to the boy; he may be chosen by the boy's parents or may volunteer for the honor anytime from the boy's birth up to the time of his circumcision. Each male in a family has a different *kirva*; there is no duplication of sponsors.

The *kirva* relationship has several basic characteristics. It is an intimate, particularistic relationship very much like kinship, but differing from it in that it is formed in a voluntary way. It is institutionalized by means of ritual and has its own reciprocal term of ritual kinship. The sponsor, who usually holds the child while the latter is being circumcised, is *kirva* to the child and his father, and vice versa. The term is often used reciprocally between members of the sponsor's and the sponsored's families. The relationship between the two families is one of trust, mutual assistance, close friendship, and respect. The rights, duties, and responsibilities between the sponsor and the child parallel those between a father and son. The sponsor shares responsibility for the boy's circumcision expenses, training, education, well-being, and marriage. In return the boy reciprocates with the loyalty, obedience, respect, and affection he gives his own father. People claim that it is more shameful to disobey or disrespect one's *kirva* than one's father.

The *kirva* relationship parallels coparenthood in another important respect: the incest taboo is extended to both families. The sponsored boy may neither marry nor have sexual relations with the offspring of his sponsor. Because of the nature of this relationship, which includes the incest taboo, the homes of both families are open to each other and the avoidance of men who are *kirva* is not observed by women of either household. Hence, the institution has both solidarity and instrumentality functions and acts as a mechanism of social control by imposing statuses and reciprocal modes of normative behavior onto the members of different kin groups.

Villagers formerly selected sponsors mainly from within Hayriye, and the *kirvalık* ties they established cross-cut quarters, kin groups, and economic statuses. People entered the relationship primarily on the basis of friendship and the desire to develop closer ties. More recently, villagers have been selecting sponsors from among Georgians living in Inegöl and in other Turkish cities. This trend appears to demonstrate an emphasis on the instrumentality function of the institution: sponsors well-situated in cities can be of greater help to a young boy hoping to escape rural life than a fellow villager can.

The structure and functions of *kirvalık* and its articulation with other elements of the social structure illustrate its adaptability to changing situations. As a mechanism for integrating previously unrelated kin groups, *kirvalık* resembles *kumstvo* as practiced in the Balkans (Hammel 1968). The subsystems of descent, affinity, and *kirvalık* are usually in complementary distribution resembling a mutually exclusive relationship among three structural allomorphs. *Kirvalık* and marriage, along with the other forms of ritual kinship to be discussed, represent structural alternatives and complements which Georgians manipulate to further organize and express a social condition whose character is in large part determined by a comparatively inflexible ideology of patrilineal descent.

A second form of spiritual kinship extant in Hayriye is called *ahret kardeşliği* (*ahret* siblingship). It is a reciprocal lifelong relationship entered into by two unrelated persons usually when they are young. *Ahret* means "the next world" and is used to designate especially close friends, who are considered inseparable in this world and in the next. If only one of the pair attains heaven, he can intercede with Allah for the other. The institution elevates friendship from the secular to the spiritual level.

Although it is most common for two boys or two girls to establish an *ahret* relationship, boy-girl pairs have been known. Generally, the relationship is formed between two youngsters who are either neighbors or classmates. They get along so well and spend so much time together, that older persons begin referring to them as *ahret* siblings. Once the community grants them this special status relationship, each begins extending reciprocal kin terms to the other's family. Such that, one will begin referring to his *ahret*'s father as "my *ahret* father," and to his *ahret*'s sister as "my *ahret* sister," and so on. In this way, two previously unrelated households enter into a spiritual kinship relationship with the rights, duties, and obligations between them being very similar to those between "real" kin. *Ahret*s are expected to help each other in times of need and to participate in each other's life cycle ceremonies. Neither may marry the other's siblings, as the relationship causes them to fall into the exogamous category. All villagers with whom I talked said they had at least one *ahret*. Commonly, *ahret*s maintain close ties into young adulthood; thereafter circumstances cause them to grow apart. Like *kirvalık*, *ahretlik* functions to extend one's personal social network and to integrate previously unrelated people. It, too, crosscuts economic statuses and village quarters.

In the past it was common for pairs of boys or young men to become blood brothers by ritualistically cutting their fingers and sucking each other's blood. However, this form of ritual kinship, which had structural features similar to those of *ahret kardeşlığı*, is no longer practiced.[10]

The Village and Its Neighborhood as Defended Spaces

Among the main concerns of all Hayriye villagers are the sanctity of their homes and the safety of their women and children. One indication of these concerns is the high fence or wall enclosing the yard adjacent to each home; another is the solidarity that village residents, especially neighbors, display to the outside. The following description applies specifically to the two or three clusters of homes in each of Hayriye's quarters which comprise what might be called "defended neighborhoods." (cf. Suttles 1972). In a more general, but less intensive way, the description is also valid for the village as a whole. That is, the entire village can also be depicted as a defended neighborhood with only slightly less solidarity than that of an immediate neighborhood.[11]

Many parts of a family's daily routine cannot be restricted to the confines of the home. While men are often away working in the fields or sitting in coffeehouses, women and children spend much of the time in their immediate neighborhood, with young ones playing in the road and women exchanging visits, fetching water from the public fountain, and walking to and from their gardens. The neighborhood becomes a communal space—a mutual extension of all households whose women and children share in its use. Within these communal spaces neighbors cooperate to maintain a high degree of security for their members. Given the nature of traditional Georgian-Muslim society, with its insistence on domestic privacy and the sanctity of women and children, such informal arrangements become necessary to govern spatial movement and to segregate categories of individuals, especially unacquainted men and women, that might otherwise confront each other, creating tension and possible conflict. A defended neighborhood is primarily a response to perceived fears of intrusion from people outside the village. Its member households share spatial propinquity and a common predicament. Most neighbors are related, either through descent, affinity, or ritual kinship. Even among those who are unrelated, the sibling attitude generated by long-time co-residence has become so ingrained that kinship terms are used among them and sexual relations would be regarded as almost incestuous.

The mutual right and obligation to protect neighbors, especially neighborhood girls, has been institutionalized in the custom of *toprak bastı* (trespass tax), which is enacted during the marriage ritual when the groom's kin fetch the bride from her parents' home. In the case of an intravillage marriage, a group of the neighborhood's young male defenders meets the procession at the edge of their territory and demands a trespass tax before allowing it to proceed. In the case of an intervillage marriage, young men from all of Hayriye's neighborhoods meet the procession at the edge of the village.

The defended neighborhood is ideally characterized by a female-dominated network of trust, cooperation and mutual aid linking its member households. When a death occurs, neighboring women look after the mourning household for at least a week; when one woman falls ill, others attend to her family until she recovers. Neighbors also materially help the poorer households among them.

Residential Quarters. After the immediate neighborhood, the next largest territory of social integration is the residential quarter (*mahalle*, Turk.). Each of Hayriye's five quarters represents a distinct spatial and social entity within a complex village whole. Quarter members share the same space, water, and roads. Each quarter elects its own member to the five-man council of elders, a body which advises the village chief. Formerly, each quarter had its own communal flour mill. More recently, however, emigration and other developments have caused all but one of these mills to fall into disrepair and disuse.

The Village. Households, immediate neighborhoods, and quarters comprise different levels of social integration which together make up the village. "Real" and ritual kinship ties interlace the village, forming diffuse bonds of respect and identification. Hayriye residents share a common pool of facts, rumors, and half-truths about each other, and they also share a collective pride and guilt over every villager's achievements and failures. Both residents and outsiders view the village as a distinct social, cultural, economic, and political entity.

Hayriye's central institutions provide the village's various webs of kinship with new uses or focal points. Among these central institutions are the village government, comprised of an elected chief (*muhtar*) and a council of elders. The chief, with the advice of the council, carries out such duties as: keeping village records, assessing a village tax (*salma*) on households, planning village projects, directing the village's communal labor (*imece*), calling meetings in which village men can discuss village problems and recommend solutions, formally and informally mediating squabbles within the village and between Hayriye and other villages, and representing the village to outside agencies.

The village mosque provides the focus for religious activity. It is the place where villagers, especially males, congregate for communal prayer and companionship and a point from which Islamic values are disseminated. The village prayer leader (*imam*) attends to the religious needs of his congregation and plays a religious role in the various life cycle rites accompanying birth, circumcision, marriage, and death. He works to promote harmony in the village, and often mediates local squabbles. His basic goal is the creation of a community of Islamic brotherhood within the community and between communities. The upkeep and repair of the mosque are the responsibility of the entire village.

Other foci of village attention and activity are the primary school, where practically all village children receive their basic, formal education; the two coffeehouses, where men from the entire village congregate periodically to discuss agricultural conditions, social topics, or anything else of interest; and, the three small village stores, which offer villagers credit and supply them with small necessities. The mosque, school, coffeehouses, and stores are all located in the village's Central Quarter.

Regional and National Integration. Like most villages in Turkey, Hayriye is bound to its nearest urban center, which in this case is Inegöl, a city of 35,000 and the seat of the sub-province. The immediate superiors of all government employees with jurisdiction in Hayriye, such as forestry officials, military police, and agricultural extension workers, maintain offices there. In turn, these offices are linked to Bursa—the provincial capital—and to Ankara, Turkey's nerve center.

Inegöl's weekly market serves as an especially important integrative mechanism, which functions simultaneously on cultural, psychological, and socioeconomic levels. It provides Hayriye's peasants with opportunities to sell their village produce, acquire cash to purchase non-village products, establish face-to-face contacts with urbanites, and increase their exposure to the outside world. Every Thursday, many Hayriye men (and a few women) travel the approximately 15 kilometers of badly eroded dirt road to Inegöl either in the back of a truck or in an overloaded minibus. To the extent possible, they try to conduct their market business on the basis of preferential relationships with other Georgians, especially former villagers who have settled in Inegöl. But in many cases, this is impossible, so they must deal with Turks and peoples of other ethnicities. In addition to buying and selling, they may visit relatives or stroll the main streets to admire the new products that are so prominently displayed in store windows. Hayriye men have a favorite coffeehouse in which they congregate and learn local, national, and international news from the more worldly wise city dwellers.

The villagers' integration with the nation is largely through travel and the country's centrally controlled and directed educational, administrative, political, military, and broadcast news systems. Some Hayriye residents have traveled to Bursa and Istanbul—the two largest cities in the Northwest. All children are obligated to attend the village school, and most do. All young men serve the required minimum of two years in the military, and practically all villagers listen to the radio, although few read newspapers. These experiences help villagers see themselves as part of a greater reality.

This chapter conceptualized the village as a system of interlocking sub-systems of different sizes and complexity which function on various levels of generality. Each subsystem consists of interacting components forming internal sources of cooperation and tension. The village's subsystems continuously interact with each other as well as with the sociocultural, economic, political, and physical dimensions of their external environment. The following chapters continue the discussion of these interactions.

NOTES

1. With respect to Georgians in the Caucasus, Grigolia (1939:60) writes: "In times past the social unit among the Georgian Highlanders, as well as among the other groups of the Georgian nation, was the joint family, called *didi-ojakhi* (*didi*—big, *ojakhi*—family)."

"The family life was conducted in one room. They slept, cooked, ate and passed their free time in discourse or other diversion openly before each other."

Like the Turks around them, the Georgians of Hayriye use the word "*aile*" for family, "*hane*" for household, and "*sülale*" for lineage. *Aile* and *sülale* derive from Arabic, *hane* derives from Persian. The word "*ojakhi*", which was used in Georgia for family, derives from Turkish.

2. For a description of the dynamics of extended household formation and fission common in Turkey, see Magnarella (1974:91).

3. The *salma* amounts have since been increased by a factor of ten, such that the highest is now TL 200 (about $14.30) and the lowest TL 20.

4. Fernea (1970:179) presents Iraqi village data, originally published by A.P.G. Poyck, that demonstrate "clearly a tendency for farm size to increase with the size of family..."

5. Referring to Georgians in the Caucasus, Grigolia writes: "The wife is subordinate to her husband, but the performance of the work of the whole household is in her hands..." (1939:58).

6. A strict Quaranic injunction for female modesty appears in Sura 24:

> And say to the believing women, that they cast down their eyes and guard their private parts, and reveal not their adornment save such as is outward; and let them cast their veils over their bosoms, and not reveal their adornment save to their husbands, or their fathers, or their husbands' fathers, or their sons, or their husbands' sons, or their brothers, or their brothers' sons, or their sisters' sons, or their women, or what their right hands own, or such men as attend them, not having sexual desire, or children who have not yet attained knowledge of women's private parts; nor let them stamp their feet, so that their hidden ornament may be known [Arberry 1955:49-50].

7. Luzbetak (1951:140) writes that in the Caucasus the Georgian "Pshavs frequently pray and offer numerous sacrifices for the blessing of a male child, and if these supernatural means fail, there is only one thing left to do—marry a second wife, who is 'capable' of giving birth to boys. At a Pshav wedding the *khevis-beri* ('The Elder of the Valley') prays: 'George, Angel of the Oak, grant thou a boy to the parents of a girl and another boy to the parents of a boy...'"

8. Referring to Georgians in the Caucasus, Grigolia (1939:57) writes: "Most of the business of choosing a bride, matchmaking and betrothal are accomplished by the parents without asking the consent of the young people." This may be somewhat exaggerated.

9. For a more comprehensive discussion of this form of ritual co-parenthood, see Magnarella and Türkdoğan (1973).

10. Certain forms of ritual kinship practiced by Georgians in the Caucasus and described by Grigolia (1939) are not present in Hayriye. Among these are such adoption rituals as anointing with consecrated oil, hair cutting, exchange of bullets, silver-eating, and "breast-biting," which "consists in touching by the candidate with his teeth the bare breast of his prospective foster mother, the wife of the head of the family, or generally the eldest woman in the family" (Grigolia 1939:16).

11. Typically, neighborhood groups in the Middle East are largely composed of patrilineal kin. For this reason, descent overlaps propinquity, and the latter's critical importance to village life is frequently overlooked. Antoun has pointed out that both in the Jordanian village he studied and among the Arab Bedouin, one of the most fundamental social units consists of that small group of related and/or unrelated people who carry out the basic functions of their survival in common or adjoining spaces (Antoun 1972).

4

Rites of Passage and Ethnotherapy

Many anthropologists use the concept "ritual" to denote any noninstinctive, predictable human action or series of actions that cannot be justified by a "rational" means-to-ends type of explanation. For example, they regard making a birthday wish a ritual, but not planting crops. Although this distinction appears simple enough on the surface, closer examination reveals serious difficulties. For one, the determination of what is "rational" and what is not, is usually culturally relative. For another, the meaning of a rite is often a mystery, even to those who enact it. Consequently, among anthropologists who specialize in the study of ritual there is wide disagreement as to the meaning of the term and the methods of understanding the symbolic content of its associated human behavior.

In their quest for understanding, some anthropologists have searched for the underlying reasons for ritual. Those following Emile Durkheim have concluded that traditional peoples with simple technologies tend to ritually reenact those parts of their lives about which they have strong (usually social) feelings. Hence, we witness hunting and fishing rituals, fertility and health rites, and so on. These they regard as magical dramatizations of ordinary social activities. James Frazer, in his voluminous work *The Golden Bough*, postulated a division of ritual into religious and magical realms. The latter, he argued, is based on the erroneous belief that false scientific techniques have the power to alter nature. By contrast, Bronislaw Malinowski asserted that religion and magic belonged to the same realm. He claimed that "man needs miracles not because he is benighted through primitive stupidity... but because he realizes at every stage of his development that the powers of his body and of his mind are limited" (Malinowski 1962:301).

More modern approaches to the study of ritual stress the idea of ritual as a special mode of communication. On one level, for example, a rite of passage can be seen as an event enacted to communicate publicly an important transition in social status. On other levels, the rite may manipulate symbols associated with the rights, duties, and responsibilities of the initiate's former and future status. The symbolic content of these and other rituals is usually intricately related, and decoding its meaning becomes an arduous task. Many theories exist as to how decoding should be accomplished (e.g., Radcliffe-Brown 1948; Lévi-Strauss 1966; Turner 1967; Geertz 1973), but none enjoys the esteem that comes with empirically proven validity.[1]

In this chapter we will remain largely on the descriptive level and offer little in the way of abstract analysis. In cases where villagers have provided an interpretation of a ritual or of an aspect of its symbolic content, we will convey that information here. However, we do not assume that current local interpretations are the reason for the ritual's origin or its persistence. In most cases, villagers claimed not to know the significance of ritual acts and justified their enactment of them simply on the grounds of tradition.

We found that most of the ritual practices we studied in Hayriye are shared by Turks in the surrounding area and in other parts of Turkey. In fact, the villagers' use of Turkish vocabulary in ritual is extensive. Although we do report on a few instances of commonality between practices and beliefs in Hayriye and those of Georgians in the Caucasus, we did not attempt a comparative study of folklife in the two areas. Nor are we able to offer a full inventory of Hayriye ritual. Instead, we will concentrate on the ritual associated with important events in a villager's life-cycle as well as the ritual comprising folk cures.

Rites of Passage

Engagement and Marriage. Most villagers believe it best to engage their daughters soon after they reach puberty. Although some young people may become acquainted, fall in love, and hope to marry a special someone, their parents usually make the final decision and arrange the marriage. This traditional system is functionally consistent with the patrilocal extended household, which was more common in the past than at present. Because a new bride customarily joined the household of her husband's parents, her selection was important to all its members and the final decision for her admittance theoretically rested with the household's patriarch. In addition, because marriage involves the alliance of two kin groups, spouse selection was to be the responsibility of mature persons who could properly evaluate the honor and reputation of potential in-laws. About the only way young couples could circumvent parental authority was, and often still is, by elopement.

Customarily, when a boy reaches his late teens, his parents initiate a search for an honorable Georgian family with a marriageable daughter. When they find such a combination, women of the two households quietly begin a series of contacts and negotiations. The boy's mother and several female relatives and/or friends visit the women of the girl's home to discuss the possibility of a marriage and inspect the potential bride. Each set of women in turn discusses the situation with their men.

Only after the women learn that both sets of men are favorably disposed to the marriage do the males actually show their hands and publicly enter the negotiations. (This is an example of how women in their private world protect male honor in the public world.) Now that the ground work has been laid, the boy's side selects two influential male relatives or friends (but not the boy's father) and the village hoja to visit the girl's father and mature male kin to request formally their consent to the marriage. Each member of the visiting party is called a *dünür* (Turk.) "intermediary."

After tea and inconsequential conversation have dissipated the meeting's initially tense atmosphere, one of the *dünürs* (usually the hoja) pronounces the standard proposal formula: "By the command of Allah and in accordance with the exalted practices of the Prophet, we wish to request your daughter for the son of our Ahmet [i.e., name of boy's father]. We accept your friendship, and would be most pleased if you accept ours." The girl's father usually replies that he and his kin will need time to discuss the proposal, but otherwise he remains noncommittal: "If Allah wills, it will be; if He does not, it will not."

Three to five days later the intermediaries return for the answer. If it is positive, the girl's father hands them a list of expectations, which includes a bridewealth of from TL 3,000 to TL 10,000 (pre-1973 figures; about $300-$1,000) and such gifts for the bride as a gold ring, gold bracelet, necklace, clothing, and household furnishings. The intermediaries accept those expectations they deem reasonable, but diplomatically try to lessen or eliminate those appearing excessive. The spacing of the events which follow—the engagement, civil wedding, and traditional religious wedding—vary greatly with individual circumstances.

Sometime after the men have concluded the proposal and bridewealth negotiations, the women of the two households hold the engagement ceremony. On an appointed evening, the groom's female kin bring part of the marital gifts to the bride's home where they dance and sing together with her female relatives and guests. The women attach paper money to the bride's dress and adorn her with bracelets and necklaces. At the height of the evening, the groom's mother places the engagement ring on the bride's finger and wishes her good fortune and happiness. Everyone congratulates the bride, and she kisses the hands of her seniors. Neither the groom nor any other male joins the gathering.

The next major event is the civil marriage ceremony, a simple and brief affair, which has been required by law in Turkey since 1926 (see Magnarella 1973). It requires the appearance of the bride and groom and two witnesses before the government wedding officer who presides in Inegöl. Friends and relatives attend this wedding, but parents customarily do not. After the ceremony is concluded, the couple returns to the village. They continue to reside in their natal homes and should not be seen together, because even though by law they are married, by custom they are still only engaged. The civil ceremony carries weight in the courts, but not in the village.

The traditional wedding ceremony, which may be held from a week to a year after the civil one, seals the marriage in the eyes of the community. It formerly consisted of a series of events spanning a week, but more recently the villagers have trimmed and streamlined the affair so that it can be conducted in two or three days.

Early in the wedding week, the bride's family sends an empty chest to the groom's home to be filled with gifts and the items agreed upon during the *dünür* negotiations. By Thursday it is returned to the bride's home and its contents, along with the bride's own prepared trousseau items (sewed and knitted things), are placed on exhibit in a room by the bride's female friends. During the next two days women from the village and from outside visit the bride's home to congratulate her and inspect the trousseau.

Wedding celebrations in the form of singing and dancing begin on Friday night when the women gather at the bride's home and men at the groom's. On the following day, after dinner and the evening prayer, villagers and other invited guests go to the groom's home where they separate into two groups by sex. The women usually gather in the home or its enclosed courtyard, while the men congregate in an open area nearby where they dance and sing to two different kinds of music. One is traditional Georgian and is played by a local accordianist and a half dozen

Fig. 6   Old men singing the "Taking the Bride" song

Fig. 7   Bride entering groom's house

village males who rhythmically beat with sticks on a plank or split log. The other, called "*alaturka*", is provided by a hired Gypsy drummer, fiddler, and clarinet player. As the men dance and sing, some of the women and girls observe them through windows or openings in the fence, while other girls dance and sing among themselves to the beat of a small drum, called *darbuka* (Arab.). Invariably, a few young men sneak off to drink raki and return energized to enliven the activities. As the night dances on, pistol shots increasingly punctuate the singing, laughter, and music.

Late that night, the merrymakers shift their location. They form a procession, led by the Gypsy musicians followed by the males and then the females, and move gayly through the village, arriving at the bride's home with a great commotion. For a brief moment the sexes intermingle; then they separate as before to continue the celebration.

While the men dance and sing outside, a group of young women—the bride's peers—engage in a special ritual. As they enter the house, each receives a piece of henna which they later apply to the bride's hands and feet. This done, they collect coins from the women present and stick as many as they can onto the bride's palms. Throughout this procedure, one or two young women play the *darbuka*, others sing and dance, and the bride weeps. Various villagers say that the henna symbolizes fertility and the coins prosperity; the merrymaking represents the joy of marriage, and the bride's weeping demonstrates the sadness associated with her forthcoming departure from her natal home.

Sometime in the early morning this part of the festivity ends. Most people go home, but a few young men overextend themselves by returning to the groom's home to continue the merriment. The next morning the bride washes off the henna and has the coins distributed to the village poor, especially to the orphans. In the past, she had her hair and make-up arranged at home; today, however, she may go to Inegöl for this. A thick coating of white facial powder gives her a sad and pathetic appearance. She then dresses in her white, European-style wedding gown, joins the women and girls already gathered in the courtyard, and dances with her peers somewhat despondently to the beat of the small drums.[2]

Throughout the morning villagers and guests from other communities arrive at the bride's home. As usual, the women and girls separate from the males. At around 1:00 p.m. all the guests are served a wedding meal consisting of rice or *bulgur* pilaf (the latter being boiled and pounded wheat) with lamb or mutton and *hoşaf* (Turk.) "a cold drink of juice containing small amounts of fruit". Whereas the villagers form groups of five or six persons and eat together around common trays, scooping up the pilaf with pieces of bread, special guests, especially those who have come great distances or who hold prominent positions in the city, are carefully served on individual plates with forks and spoons. Although this meal is served at the bride's home, the expense falls on the groom's family. Neighbors and friends help out by cooking and lending trays, dishes, glasses, pots, and other utensils.

That same morning the groom breakfasts at his own home with a group of his male peers. Shortly after finishing, a barber arrives to perform the "shaving of the groom" ritual. Once his week's growth of beard has been removed, the groom dresses in the modern, European-style suit sent to him by the bride's family. During the shaving and dressing, both of which are conducted in the inner courtyard on a colorful kilim, the young men joke, dance, and sing to music provided by the hired Gypsy musicians.

At about 3:00 or 4:00 in the afternoon, a group of men from the groom's side go to pick up the bride. In the past, they transported her on a horse; then during the 1950s and 1960s they hired a taxi; now they commonly use a car brought back from Germany by one of the village's vacationing workers. Their arrival at the bride's home is the signal for the young lady to go to the kitchen and bid farewell to her relatives who are gathered by the hearth. She embraces her mother and father, and they wish her happiness and prosperity and advise her to be a good *gelin* (Turk.) "bride" or "new wife". Before she is permitted to cross the threshold and leave the home, her siblings block the way and demand money from the groom's party. After they make this payment, called *kapı harcı* (Turk.) "door customs", the bride exits. (This customs has been as high as several thousand liras, $300-$400.). Two men from the groom's party vertically hold up a sheet or spread near the car door so that the bride may get in without being seen by the evil or envious eye. She enters the car right foot first, while someone nearby recites a Quranic prayer. A young married woman, who has acted as the bride's guide throughout the week, sits next to her. This guide, called *ahret*,[3] is commonly a sister-in-law or a young affinal aunt. She must be someone that the bride can confide in and receive marital instructions from without experiencing embarrassment.

As the bridal car begins to move away, several women throw water after it from copper jugs and yell out, "*Beteketli gitsin*" (Turk.) "may she be fertile, abundant", and the bride's father throws candy behind it so that the marriage may go sweetly. Then the bridal procession moves slowly through the village: Gypsy musicians first, followed by the men and boys, then the bridal car, with the women and girls last. If the bride is being taken away from Hayriye, a group of boys and young men usually prevents the car from leaving the village until the groom's party has paid them an exit fee. The same group would have already stopped the car when it entered the village and demanded a trespass payment (Turk."*yer bastı para*"). If the bride is being taken to another quarter of the village, the same happens when the car is about to cross a quarter boundary. The procession continues on slowly, stopping frequently as the males sing and dance along the way.

When the car finally enters the groom's courtyard, his father commonly throws hard candy and coins (representing sweetness and prosperity) into the air and children scramble about to retrieve them. The old men at the head of the procession join together to sing a Georgian song called "the taking of the bride" (see Figure 6). Then a male fires a full pistol load into the chimney, and the young men have a turn at singing the "taking of the bride" song. The car now approaches the home entrance and stops. As before, two men hold up a sheet or spread vertically and the bride is helped out of the car and led to the door while everyone applauds. At this point, the groom comes out of the house, and puts an arm around his bride's waist. Together they enter the home under crossed knives or daggers held above the threshold by two men (see Figure 7). After they have entered, these men cut away several slivers from the top of the wooden threshold. (Some villagers informed me that this symbolized the cutting away of any evil or misunderstandings that may have existed, so that the couple may begin their marital lives free from those kinds of burdens.)[4]

Someone then leads a sheep or goat around the car three times. In the past this animal was sent to the bride's parents, who slaughtered it and prepared a meal of trotters for wedding guests on the next day, which they call *paça günü* (Turk.) "trotters day". Even though the villagers have eliminated the trotters day custom from the wedding ritual, someone still circles the animal around the car. My informants did not know what, if anything, the ritual symbolized. They simply explained it as custom.

The groom takes his bride into the *gerdek odası* (Turk.) "nuptial chamber" and presents her with a gift, usually a bracelet. He then goes outside to embrace and thank his friends for providing so much help, gaiety, and emotional support throughout the week.

The women of the household then take the bride to the kitchen where she is seated on a chair and a small boy, who is unrelated to her, is placed on and off her lap three times, so that she may give birth to a son of her own. Next she removes her wedding gloves and kneads wheat flour and water. She then either presses her right hand to the wall above the hearth, leaving its print there, or wipes it on the hem of her mother-in-law's skirt. (Village women told me that the hand wiping on the skirt is done to make the bride obedient to her mother-in-law.)[5]

That evening the women and girls gather at the groom's home for singing, dancing, additional ritual, and a meal of rice pilaf, meat, *hoşaf*, and a special bread (Turk. *"katma ekmeği"*) containing walnuts. The bride's mother and her close patrilateral female relatives do not attend. During the evening the bride's brother and two male companions (usually close patrilateral kin) enter the groom's home for the Georgian veil raising ritual. The brother playfully lifts and drops the bride's veil several times with the tip of his sword and asks the groom's mother what she plans to give his sister now that she has joined her household. The groom's mother may answer seriously or jokingly, extravagantly or simply. She may merely respond, "I have given her my son. What else can I do?" The brother then plunges his sword into a cauldron in which a raw chicken has been placed on top of three to five *katmer*s (Turk.) "flaky pastries with sugared walnuts". He tries to pierce the chicken and all that is below it, because he may keep all that comes out on his sword. This done, the brother and his companions leave.

The women now call for the groom and coax him to dance while they clap and sing. Shy and embarrassed, he quickly leaves, and his mother then lifts the bride's veil permanently. She has the bride respectfully kiss her hand and then she throws out candy to all present. The guests congratulate the bride and pin money (commonly 10 lira bills) onto her gown, while someone places a gold bracelet on her wrist.

During this evening, also, one representative and one witness each from both the groom's and the bride's side gather together in the groom's home to perform the religious marriage ritual. All participants are male adults, but neither the groom nor the bride's father is present. They begin the ceremony after eating dinner. The two parties kneel on the floor side by side with the *imam* kneeling opposite them so that the groom's party is on his right—the favored side. The *imam* thrusts a knife into the floor in the midst of the group, and everyone places his hands on his knees to pray to Allah for the forgiveness of their misdeeds. This prayer, like the cutting away of wood slivers from the threshold, is done to give the marriage a clean start.

The *imam* turns to the bride's representative and says, "In the name of Allah and in accordance with the exalted traditions of the Prophet, you have been named representative of Mehmet's [i.e., the bride's father's] daughter." The *imam* then asks three times: "By Allah's command, did you give this girl?" The representative responds three times: "By the power of my office as representative, I gave her." Next, the *imam* turns to the groom's representative and asks: "By Allah's command, did you take this girl?" He, too, responds affirmatively three times. The *imam* then says, "Amen," and together they recite the *Fatiha* —the opening chapter of the *Quran*. They end the ceremony by drinking *şerbet* (Turk.) "a sweet fruit drink" and praying that the newlyweds' lives may pass happily and sweetly. The group then departs.

Late that night the groom returns home and joins his bride in the nuptial chamber. They pray together and then consummate the marriage. In Hayriye, as in practically all of the Muslim World, virginity and male honor are closely associated. A single girl must preserve her viginity so as not to stain the honor of her male kin and her future husband. In order to demonstrate to the community that this honor is intact, Hayriye villagers observe the common Muslim custom of sending the nuptial sheet to the home of the bride's family on the morning following the marriage's consummation. According to tradition, blood stains on the sheet prove the bride had maintained her virginity up until her marriage night. Unstained sheets, however, mean she has tainted her husband's and her family's honor. In such a case, she can be sent back to her family and the marriage declared void. But in Hayriye, according to informants, the sheet is always stained!

In years past, an additional event took place on the evening the bride was taken to the groom's home. Although the villagers say it is a Georgian custom, they refer to it by a Turkish name—*sofra tutulması* "capturing the table". On this evening, some of the bride's male kin went to the groom's home for dinner. Singing to music, they ordered all kinds of exotic foods and dishes, for example specially prepared fish or fruit which was out of season. In order to find these foods, the groom's kin had to travel to neighboring villages or Inegöl. Even then they often were unable to meet the demands of their affinal guests and consequently experienced embarrassment. After dinner, the guests, if satisfied, danced to the same music they had used to sing out their dinner orders. Hayriye informants told me that this ritual was so demanding, that the villagers dropped it by consensus.

On Monday, a group of the bride's female peers gather together with her to perform what clearly appears to be a fertility and harmony ritual. The bride dresses in her wedding gown and arranges her hair. Her peers spread a sheet or bedspread on the floor, and the bride places wheat, barley, and/or corn seed mixed with sugar on the sheet in rows as if she were planting them. Meanwhile, someone in the group reads or recites an Islamic prayer.

During the week following the marriage's consummation, the couple and the bride's family practice mutual avoidance. At the end of that week, the bride and groom, accompanied by their wedding guides—the bride's *ahret* and the groom's *sağdıç* —go to the home of the bride's parents for dinner. Villagers call this custom *ayak dönüşü* (Turk.) "foot return". First, the bride enters, saying *bismillah* (Arab.) "in the name of Allah", and kisses the hands of her senior kin to demonstrate respect. She and the women then go to a separate room where they sit, talk, and later eat dinner. Next, someone fires a pistol shot to announce the groom. He enters, also saying *bismillah*, and is greeted by the senior men of the house, whose hands he kisses. The men then move to a different room where they converse and eat. The family has the *Mevlut* —the poem written by Suleyman Çelebi depicting the birth of Mohammad—read either before or after dinner. This meeting "opens the way"; henceforth, both parties may exchange visits freely, and the couple may carry on as ordinary villagers.

Birth. Because the various rituals and observations associated with pregnancy and childbirth lay within the private cultural domain of women and normally should not be discussed with men, a male anthropologist experiences difficulty collecting such information. Fortunately however, two village women were willing to supply me with the following.

The Georgians of Hayriye condone early pregnancies (after the first nine months) and value large families. Every couple prays for children. Although they prefer boys, there is no evidence of female infanticide, which reportedly existed among the nineteenth century Georgian mountaineers of the Caucasus (Kuipers 1956b:531). A woman who has not given birth, especially to a son, feels inferior to those who have. She may take recourse to folk or ethno-religious remedies; more recently, she may visit a doctor as well.

Villagers regard pregnancy as a time of joy, as well as extreme caution. The expectant mother becomes subject to a series of taboos to protect herself and her child. For instance, she should not come face to face with another pregnant woman or an expectant animal for fear that some physical or mental impairment may result to herself or her child.

Village women normally deliver in their own homes with the aid of a local midwife, who maintains a life-long attachment to the mother and child. On the day of birth the midwife gives the child his (her) temporary name. This is an Islamic name which she whispers in his right ear three times along with the *sala* (Arab.) "the chant from the minaret on the occasion of the Friday prayer". For boys she commonly whispers either Ahmet or Mehmet, for these are derived from Mohammad. For girls she whispers Aisha (the name of Mohammad's favorite wife, called the mother of believers) or Fatma (from Fatima—Mohammad's daughter). The child receives his second or permanent appellation on the third day when his family customarily names him after a grandparent or other relative several generations removed.

A week after a woman's first child is born (especially if it is a boy), she, her female relatives and friends hold a celebration, referred to as *poppioba* (Georg.). Villagers claim this is a Georgian custom; Turks in the area appear not to practice it. All the women gather at the new mother's home to dine on rice pilaf and mutton from a ram specially sacrificed for the occasion. For dessert they have *kaçama* (Turk.) "pudding made of either corn or wheat flour". The guests sing and dance to express their joy and present the mother with gifts. The mother's mother customarily uses the occasion to bring her grandchild his cradle, mattress, blankets, and sheets.

If the first child is a girl or if the family experienced a tragedy around the time of birth, they usually postpone the *poppioba* until the next child is born. For example, one mother told me that on the occasions of her first two births (both were daughters), two of her elderly relatives had just died. Consequently, she did not have the *poppioba* until the birth of her third child—a boy. Then, her family was so overjoyed that they sacrificed several sheep and had a gala affair.

During the first forty days after birth both the mother and child exist in an endangered state. Throughout this period, and for several years to come, a mother pins or sews a special blue bead onto her child's clothing to protect him from the evil eye. The mother must again observe many taboos. Because she may hemorrhage during this period, she should not cook for others, if at all possible, because the flowing blood puts her in an impure state. She should not eat hot foods, such as pepper or onion, for these may affect her child through her milk, causing a rash to break out on his face.[6] Nor should she come face to face with a woman or animal that also recently gave birth, for such an encounter may impair her child's ability to walk.

One woman told me that she had had such an encounter during her forty days, and later her child could not walk on time. She called a village woman, who knows prayers and cures, and had her wash the child and say prayers over him on three consecutive Saturdays. This cured him. Other women have special persons come and perform a lead melting ritual (see "Ethnotherapy" below). My informants said village mothers usually see good results from these practices, and if they do not, they now consult a doctor.

Both the mother and child should avoid strangers, and neither should visit another home. They should always be accompanied or guarded by close female relatives or friends. If for any reason the person looking after them must leave them alone, she should place either a broom or an iron poker against the wall next to the door. The broom is associated with cleaning and the iron strength; both have the power to obstruct the entrance of evil spirits, who are associated with filth.[7] The experiencing of adversity by the mother or child during these first forty days is referred to as *kırka karışır* (Turk.) "mixing or confusing the forty days."

On the fortieth day, the mother bathes herself and her child. This ritual ablution, called *kırklama* (Turk.) "passing forty days", represents a cleansing of impurities and an emergence from confinement. They are now freed of the forty-day taboos and the dangers associated with them.

Circumcision. The background to and the social relationships resulting from the circumcision (Arab. "*sünnet*") custom have already been discussed in Chapter III. Here we will concentrate on the associated ritual.

Customarily, when a boy reaches six or seven, his family begins arranging for his circumcision celebration. They start by searching for a circumcision sponsor (called *kirva*), who will become the boy's spiritual father and the boy his spiritual son. They then set a date for sometime after harvest and invite fellow villagers as well as relatives and friends who have moved to the city.

On circumcision day, men and women go to the boy's house and gather in separate rooms to recite the *Mevlut* with the help of the local *imam* and/or a *hafiz* (Arab.) "one who has memorized the *Quran*". Meanwhile the boy, who wears a special white suit and hat, is paraded around the village in a rented taxi (formerly on horseback) accompanied by his male peers and led by hired Gypsy musicians, whose music announces the event and the procession.

Ideally, the *Mevlut* recitation and the procession end almost simultaneously, and men bring the boy home saying, "*Allah ekber*" (Arab.) "God is most great" as they come. They take him to the men's room, where they remove his suit and hat, and dress him in a night gown. Then, while the *kirva* holds the boy's arms from behind and others hold his legs, the circumciser quickly cuts the foreskin. Men try to distract the boy by loudly repeating, "God is most great!" The boy's penis is bandaged as the men compliment him for displaying a lion's bravery. They place the boy in a bed specially decorated with a silk quilt and colorful ribbons, and individually pass by to congratulate him and place money (10 to 100 lira bills) by his side. They are followed by the women, who also give money, and then the children.

Villagers do not consider circumcision a ritual that makes boys adults. They do believe, however, that a boy should be circumcised before he reaches twelve, for from that age on he is obligated to say the daily prayers and enters the men's part of the mosque. Prior to that, he commonly stays with the women in the balcony. Hence, one might think of circumcision as a ritual initiation into the male realm, but not into manhood. For girls, there appears to be no corresponding ritual and daily prayers become obligatory at age nine.

Death. When it becomes evident that an ailing person is approaching death, his or her relatives, close friends and the village *imam* gather in his room to pray. They have the dying person repent for his sins and ask for Allah's forgiveness. Then, without alarming him they help him bequeath his worldly possessions. First attention is given to the soul, by assigning money to the poor, the village mosque, and the local school. Then the failing one may recognize the rights of his kin before witnesses.

Periodically the *imam* and others repeat the profession of the faith: "There is no God but Allah, and Mohammad is his Prophet." They do not ask the dying one to say it, for if he should not be able to complete the formula (especially, if he should stop after saying, "There is no god . . . ."), he might die without his faith. Those near him also read the *Ya Sin*, the 36th *sura* of the *Quran*, hoping to reduce his pain. Someone wets a piece of cotton with clean water and uses it to quench the failing one's thirst, for villagers believe the Devil comes to dying persons (who are all extremely thirsty) and offers them a drink of water in exchange for their faith.[8]

Once the person passes away, he (she) is taken from his bed and laid on a kilim such that he faces the direction of Mecca. His clothes are removed; his chin is tied closed with a piece of white cotton cloth; his big toes are bound together with cotton string; and his arms are rested by his side. If he dies with his eyes open, they are gently shut, and those near him say that he died longing to see a loved one. His nude body is then wrapped in a white sheet and a knife is placed on his chest. Some informants say the knife is to prevent swelling, but Georgians also believe iron has the strength to drive off evil spirits

The next morning the village *imam* comes to the home of the deceased to read the entire *Quran*. He also collects the "soul money" bequeathed the previous day and sees that it goes to the intended recipients. Then the body is taken outside for the *taharet* "canonical purification". In Hayriye, the village *imam* washes males, and a local woman washes females. Here, as in other parts of Turkey, the woman who ritually washes corpses should not also perform the duties of a midwife, for the mixing of birth and death categories is prohibited. Analogously, as fuel to heat the water used in this ritual ablution, villagers commonly use beech, oak, or other deciduous tree wood, rather than the wood of evergreens which are associated with life, not death.

As the ritual ablution takes place, relatives may burn incense in the deceased's home to purify it and attract the angels. After the corpse has been ritually washed three times, camphored pieces of cotton are put in all its orifices and between its joints. The corpse is then placed in a shroud, which has been sprinkled with camphor and black cumin seeds. Then the shroud is tied at head and foot and the corpse is rested in a wooden coffin.

This done, relatives, friends, and the *imam* gather at the deceased's home. First they pray, then four to six men pick up the coffin on their shoulders to carry it to the village mosque. They stop and start three times in front of the deceased's home before getting underway. As they move along the village roads, members of the all male procession take turns carrying the coffin in order to show their respect for the dead and earn *sevap*—Allah's reward for a pious act.

Upon arriving at the mosque, they place the coffin on the funeral stone "*musalla taşı*" outside and enter to say the afternoon prayer "*öğle namazı*". They then return outside for the funeral prayer "*cenaze namazı*". After reading the *Fatiha* "the opening chapter of the Quran", the *imam* addresses the gathering and they respond as follows:

Imam: "Venerable gathering, how did you know this man (or woman)?"
Gathering: "We knew him to be good."
Imam: "Will you act as witnesses to his virtue on the Day of Judgement?"
Gathering: "Yes, we will."
Imam: "Neighbors, give up your claims over this person."
Gathering: "They are given up."

They then carry the coffin on their shoulders to the cemetery, taking turns and being careful not to look back as they go, for many villagers believe backward glances would cause another death in the community. According to the village *imam*, there is a *hadith* (Arab.) "tradition of the prophet" to the effect that the deceased sees those who wash him, take him to the grave, and participate in his funeral.

At the cemetery they set the coffin on the ground next to the prepared grave. They then take the corpse out and place it in the grave such that it reclines on its back and right shoulder and faces the direction of Mecca. Should the deceased be a female, those who place her in the grave should be male relatives within the prohibited decrees of marriage. Participation by others would cause defilement.

They place boards above the body and fill in the rest of the grave with dirt. The *imam* again reads the *Ya Sin* and leads the assembled in prayer. When they have finished, a senior male relative of the deceased rises and thanks those present by saying, "*Hepinizin başınız sağ olsun*" (Turk.) "May your lives be spared". They reply, "*Sağ ol*" (Turk.) "May you be well and strong."

The group then departs; only the *imam* remains to perform the *Telkin* (Arab.) "final rites" which include instructions for the deceased. Should he be asked his god, he should respond, "Allah"; his religion is Islam, and his book is the *Quran*. Some villagers believe that when the *imam* finishes the *Telkin*, the deceased tries to sit up in his grave. In the process he bumps his head on the boards above him and realizes for the first time that he is truly dead.

For seven nights after the burial female relatives and friends go to the home of the deceased where they join his female kin in prayer and a reading of the *Ya Sin*. Villagers believe that on the 52nd night, the deceased's flesh separates from his bones and he suffers immensely. As a consequence, his family calls the village *imam* to their home on the 52nd night and the two nights prior to it to have him recite a special "52nd night prayer" which implores Allah to ease or eliminate the deceased's pain. The *imam* recites this prayer in Arabic seven times on each night for a total of 21 recitations. In addition, women gather annually on the night of burial to read the *Quran* and *Mevlut* for the deceased.

All of the rituals and beliefs described above are shared by Turks throughout the country (cf. Ornek 1971) and are associated with grief and mourning. The only death ritual practiced in Hayriye which I found to be unique (i.e., not shared by Turks, and probably uniquely Georgian) is the following. Should the deceased be a family patriarch, a wooden post is placed in the ground under his house directly beneath his body. It remains there until shortly after the corpse is removed. (If the home's construction prevents the post from being situated under it, it is placed next to the home's entrance.) Villagers told me that they did not know the meaning of this custom, but thought it feasible that in the past the post might have symbolized the patriarch's supportive role.

Ethnotherapy

Every society institutionalizes responses to the human illnesses which are regular consequences of a people's relationship with their sociocultural and natural environments. The people of Hayriye, like the members of all human groups, share (more or less) a body of belief concerning the nature of illness, its etiology and cure, and its place within the system of social relations.

In addition to the natural causes of illness, villagers believe *nazar* (Turk.) "the evil eye", *büyü* (Turk.) "sorcery", and *cin şerri* (Turk.) "evil spirits" or "demons" are separate causes, especially of those illnesses which do not respond to scientific treatment. The therapeutic practices employed for the treatment of illnesses brought about by these sources include elements of religion (especially as reintegrated by the "Little Tradition"), sympathetic magic, and both proscribed and prescribed social behavior. When treatment requires a specialist, he (or she) and the patient usually enter into a reciprocal and ritualistic psychosocial relationship

Formerly practically everyone in Hayriye relied on home remedies and folk curers for relief from their sickness and ailments. During the 1950s, however, one male villager succeeded in becoming a medical doctor, and more recently he established his office in Istanbul. This development has encouraged villagers to combine their traditional therapeutic procedures with those of modern medicine. Many take recourse to local cures and in addition travel to Istanbul to be examined by the doctor from Hayriye.

They would rather make the long trip to consult with a familiar person than visit an unknown doctor in nearby Inegöl. The doctor's older brother, who still resides in Hayriye, describes him as "a savior of a doctor. The very sick go to him, and if their day has not yet come, he saves them." This statement reveals a blending of traditional fatalism (especially a belief in *ecel*—the appointed hour of death) and an awe for the ability of a modern doctor. Rather than fully replace customary remedies, modern medicine has added to the range of therapies that local people utilize.

In Hayriye, as throughout Turkey, men and women who allegedly possess a special power to cure are called either *ocaklı* (Turk.) "guild member" or *izinli* (Turk.) "one with permission". When such a person becomes very old, he or she transmits the power to another so that it will not be lost. During the ritual of transmission, the *ocaklı* person holds the other's hands and recites a formula which passes the power through the hands and permits the other to cure. In addition, because the belief in the efficacy of Quranic words is so strong, many villagers regard almost anyone who can either read the *Quran* or recite portions of it as a potential curer.

Even though the practice of folk medicine is widespread, Turkish law prohibits it and the urban elite criticize it severely. Consequently, many villagers discuss these practices with great reluctance. I collected descriptions of the following eight practices from two middle-aged village women and one of their teenaged daughters. These curing procedures are very common in Turkey (cf. Bayri 1947:91-113), and Hayriye villagers refer to them by their Turkish names. The following represent only a fraction of the villagers' entire inventory of folk therapies.

Kursun Dökmek "pouring lead". If a child does not begin to walk when he normally should, villagers believe his mother must have confronted a female animal that had given birth during the first forty days following the woman's own delivery. Her female relatives or close friends call a *okuyucu kadın* (Turk.) "reading woman", who is commonly one who can recite Quranic verses and may be considered *izinli* as well. On three consecutive Saturdays the curer performs the same ritual. She places a small amount of lead into a metal ladle and melts it over a fire. She then holds a bowl of water above the head of the subject child and pours the melted lead into it, saying as she does: "[I do this] not with my hand, but with the hand of my mother Aisha Fatma." (Aisha was the Prophet Mohammad's favorite wife and is known as the mother of believers.)[9] Supposedly, as the lead cools, its shape depicts the form of the animal that confronted the child's mother. Next, the curer washes the child with the water that cooled the lead, beginning with his head and finishing with his feet. She then dampens the ashes of the fire used to melt the lead and wraps them in a piece of cotton cloth. This she places under the child's mattress or pillow overnight. She returns each Sunday morning to break open the dried and hardened ashes and shows that they contain hair from the confronted animal. In the process, the curer reportedly breaks the evil spell over the child and remedies him. My informants asserted that many Hayriye mothers found this therapy effective.

Ateş Söndürmek."extinguishing a fire" or "reducing a fever". This curing ritual is performed somewhat similarly to *kurşun dokmek*, but an *ocaklı* or *izinli* person is not required. Should a member of a family become sick with a fever (Turk. "*ateş*") that is believed to have been caused by the evil eye, any senior female member of the household can apply this remedy. She takes three hot pieces of charcoal from the brazier and drops them into a bowl of water held first over the feverish person's head, then his or her midsection, and lastly his feet. As she drops the coals into the water she says, "In the name of Allah. [I do this] not with my hand, but with the hand of Aisha Fatma." This involves a form of sympathetic magic and symbolic transference. For as the fire "*ateş*" is extinguished, the fever "*ateş*" is supposed to subside.

Şerbet Dökmek: "to pour a sweet fruit drink". When an individual is troubled by a *ruh* "soul", *akil* "mental", or *sinir* "nervous" disorder which is associated with or follows a fall, his family believes evil spirits are the underlying cause and must be propitiated before health can be restored. Either the ill person, himself, or a member of his family prepares a sweet fruit drink (Turk. "*şerbet*") in the ordinary fashion. Then a person who can either read or recite the *Quran* comes to the home and says the *Sure-i Ihlas*—112th *sura* of the *Quran*—three times and the *Fatiha* once. Next, he blows over the *şerbet*. At about midnight, the ill person secretly takes the sweet drink either to the spot where he presumably collided with evil spirits and fell, or to a crossroad where he pours it on the ground, saying, "Take my troubles, give me my health. We give flavor to your mouth, give flavor to ours in return" (i.e., we please you, please us in return). The ill person must then return home quickly without looking back.

In a somewhat similar fashion, villagers have traditionally attempted to propitiate evil spirits when they move into a new home. They ritually pour *şerbet* under the stairs or in the corner of the basement, believing that these demons, who live in dark, dirty areas or where people are likely to fall, will be pleased and as a result not create trouble.

Dalak Kesmek "to cut the spleen". This formerly popular cure for serious cases of malaria (uncommon in Hayriye today) must be performed by an *izinli* person. The curer procures a sheep's spleen and places it on the sick person's stomach. He and the patient then go through the following ritual questions and answers three times:

> Patient: What are you cutting? Curer: I am cutting [name of the sick person]...'s spleen. Patient: If that is so, cut it. Curer: I cut it, and it went away.

With each repetition of the above, the curer cuts across the spleen with a black handled knife. He then gives the spleen to the patient who hangs it next to the oven in his home. Villagers believe that as the spleen dries and shrinks from the heat of the oven, the patient's own spleen (which has swelled from malaria) will return to normal size and he will recover.

Sarılık Kesmek: "to cut jaundice". When a person becomes jaundiced, members of his family may take him to an *izinli* woman in the village, who specializes in a ritual cure for this condition. On three consecutive Saturdays this woman recites a prayer (which was not known by my informants) and makes a small cut between the patient's eyebrows with a razor or sharp knife just enough to draw blood.

Informants also said that a special *hoja* in Inegöl cures jaundice by cutting under the patient's tongue and then putting either garlic or onion on the wound (cf. Bayrı 1947:94).

Tütsülemek:"to fumigate". Villagers commonly use fumigants as remedies for human or animal illness believed to have been caused by the evil eye. They place garlic, harmal seeds, black cumin, corn flour, and small slivers of wood from the threshold of their home's entrance either singly or in a combination in a metal container to burn. They then hold the container near the sick person or animal so that he (it) may breathe in the fumes and recover.

Quranic Verses and Prayers. As mentioned earlier, villagers assign great power to Quranic words, whether they are read, written, or recited. One of the most commonly employed ethnotherapies is a Quranic reading or recitation. The following case was related to me by a village woman in her thirties.

> When a person gets a fever and hallucinates, we know he has collided with an evil spirit. My son often has such a fever. He closes his eyes and cries out, "Mommy, they're coming! The hojas are coming!" He also shivers and trembles. He does this about twice a year, usually after midnight. We asked our Istanbul doctor about this, and he said they were infantile convulsions. But we say evil spirits and have the hoja come to read the *Quran*. Then the condition passes quickly.

I observed the following case in the home of the Hayriye village *imam* on a morning during the summer of 1972. It is related here from field notes:

When I arrived at the *imam*'s home by previous invitation, his son met me at the gate and showed me to the sitting room. Inside the *imam* was conversing with a Georgian village male of about 30-35 years, who was employed in Germany, but was home on vacation. As I deduced from their conversation this man had brought his wife and mother-in-law with him to Germany where they lived together. While there his mother-in-law had fainted several times on the same spot. He had taken her to doctors, but they could find nothing wrong. Now, he was asking the *imam* for a remedy. The *imam* listened and read in Arabic from a thin book which he later said was *Ayet-i Kerime* "sacred verse" sent by Allah to restore health. He asked the man questions about his mother-in-law: "Does she see water in her dreams? Does she experience anxiety?" He then began writing Quranic verses in Arabic on three or four long, narrow slips of paper. He carefully folded each slip into a small triangle, tucking the end into the last opening like an envelope. Each was a *muska* "amulet". He told the man that his mother-in-law should keep one or two of these *muska*s on her person; the rest should be buried "nearby." He also told the man to collect water from seven fountains in the village and mix it with *nar suyu* (Turk.) "promegranate juice". He recommended that he go to a pharmacy and buy a brand medicine called Passiflora. (I later went to a pharmacy to inquire about this medicine and learned that it is recommended for anxiety, insomnia, and emotional neuroses.) The *imam* said these should be taken to Germany and the woman should drink a portion of either the fountain water mixed with pomegranate juice or the Passiflora before each meal.

He also told the man to collect dust from the spot in Germany where his mother-in-law had repeatedly fainted, and then mix it with either black cumin or harmal seeds and make a fumigant from the result. When the *imam* finished, the man thanked him and made an offer of money. But the *imam* refused any payment, so the man thanked him again and left.

When I asked the *imam* about this case, he became quite embarrassed, and tried to pass it off as a midwife remedy that he recommends only because it is customary. He stressed the fact that in addition to the midwife remedy, he also recommended Passiflora, a modern medicine. He said he was confident that the latter would bring about good results.

NOTES

1. For an excellent discussion of some of the conceptual and theoretical

problems associated with the determination of symbolic meaning in the Islamic world, see el-Zein (1977).

2. I visited other Georgian villages in this region and witnessed brides dancing on this occasion with their married male relatives. In Hayriye, however, women dance exclusively among themselves. This apparently results from their greater assimilation of Turkish culture.

3. *Ahret* (Turk.) means "the next world" and is used reciprocally by close female friends, who consider themselves inseparable in this world and in the next. The groom's corresponding intimate, who acts as guide and companion throughout the wedding week, is called *sağdıç* (Turk.).

4. Grigolia's descriptions of wedding ritual among the Christian Georgian Highlanders of the Caucasus parallel mine in several interesting respects. Compare the following by Grigolia:

> in the giving of the bride by her people as well as her acceptance by the kinsmen of the groom, group solidarity and sustenance of mutual interests are clearly expressed. The whole community of the bride bids her good-bye at her departure, and on the other side all kindred of the groom welcome her" [1939:74].

> to keep the evil spirits away, the attendants and friends of the bride and groom fire their guns during the time of leaving the church after the wedding, and on the way to the groom's house, and particularly before entering the house. As protection against the same danger, it is customary for the married couple to pass under crossed sabres when leaving the door of the church [1939:74].

Grigolia writes that the bride also passes under crossed daggers when she first enters the groom's home (1939:88). In Hayriye, the customs of firing a pistol into the chimney and passing under crossed daggers appear to be derived from Georgian rather than Turkish sources.

5. The interfamilial negotiations to arrange the marriage, the bridewealth practice, the absence of the groom during most of the wedding celebrations, and the use of sugar or honey to ensure that the couple's lives will be sweet have also been reported for the Georgian Highlanders in the Caucasus by Grigolia (1939). In addition, the following description of Christian Georgian customs practiced in Caucasia resembles what has been observed in Hayriye:

> The marriage customs of the Georgians are regulated by Christianity. ...After the ceremony in the church the wedding is celebrated publicly in the house of the bride; the feast may last several days. Then the bride is brought to the house of the groom in a noisy

procession on horseback. She is welcomed by her mother-in-law who puts a lump of sugar or other sweets in her mouth; then she is led around the hearth, and a male child is put on her knee to ensure fecundity [Kuipers 1956b:534].

6. Formerly Hayriye mothers breastfed their children for one to two years; more recently, however, they have been doing so for only four or five months. They attributed the robustness of their children to a mixture of corn flour, butter, and milk, which they traditionally began feeding them about ten days after birth. Now, more and more mothers are relying on commercially prepared baby foods.

7. Turks also observe these customs. The belief in the power of iron to drive away evil spirits also existed among Georgians in the Caucasus (Grigolia 1939:106-107).

8. These beliefs and practices are widespread in Turkey and throughout much of the Middle East. For instance, Donaldson (1938:70-71) writes the following about the Shiite Muslims of Iran:

The specially prepared Korans which have marginal notes, have written alongside the sura 'Ya Sin,' that every Muslim should either read this sura himself, or have it read to him, at the time of his death. This will ease the pain, calm the fears, and make the 'soul-taking' bearable, and for every letter that is pronounced in the reading ten angels will descend and stand before him in order, and they will pray for his forgiveness. At the washing of his body they will also be present, and they will follow after the bier in the procession, and will attend his burial. Also his spirit will not leave the body until an angel of Paradise appears and gives him some of the heavenly sherbet to drink, then after he has satisfied his thirst, Azra'il will take his spirit. In the grave he will not thirst, and on the day of resurrection he will not need the water which the prophets will have ready for him.

9. Interestingly, my informants equated Aisha with Mary, the mother of Christ, and referred to her as "our mother Mary." This illustrates how the "Little Tradition" of the peasant community reintegrates the "Great Tradition".

5
Economy,
Material Culture,
and Society

This chapter describes Hayriye's economy, especially as it existed in 1961-62; later chapters discuss more recent changes. Information comes primarily from the Middle East Technical University study (referred to as *Hayriye Köy Araştırma* 1963) and my own field notes which consist of interview and observational data recorded in 1970, 1972, and 1974.

Before beginning, a cautionary note is called for. Villagers in Hayriye, as in many other parts of the world, work scattered plots of irregular shape and fertility. Rarely do they accurately measure and record the economic factors related to their farms, and as a result their assessments of crop acreage and yields are often only rough estimates. Hence, many of the figures presented below can be regarded as useful approximations at best.

The Homestead

In Hayriye a complete and ideal homestead is composed of a house (*ev*), an elevated corn shed (*bagen*), a granary (*ambar*), a straw shed (*samanlık*), and a stable (*ahır*) (see Figure 8). The design and function of these buildings both provide the focal points of a family's social and economic life and

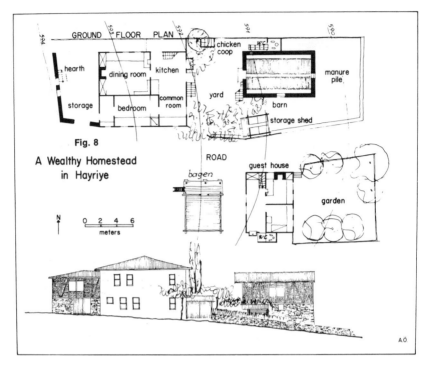

GROUND FLOOR PLAN

hearth
storage
dining room
kitchen
bedroom
common room
chicken coop
yard
barn
storage shed
manure pile

Fig. 8

A Wealthy Homestead in Hayriye

N

0 2 4 6
meters

ROAD

bagen

guest house

garden

A.Ö.

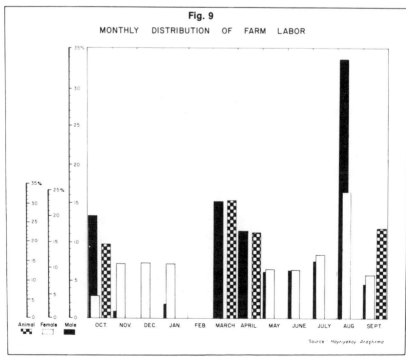

Fig. 9

MONTHLY DISTRIBUTION OF FARM LABOR

35%

30

25

20

15

10

5

OCT. NOV. DEC. JAN. FEB. MARCH APRIL MAY JUNE JULY AUG. SEPT.

Animal Female Male

Source *Hayriyeköy Araştırma*

reveal the temporal order of work and the disposition of the fruits of labor.

Practically all village homes are two-story structures composed of stone foundation, timber frames with adobe bricks piled between them to form the walls, a mud plaster covering on the interior walls, an optional covering on the exterior walls, and a crown of red tile (see Figure 11). Villagers commonly whitewash or blue the walls, and women weave rush mats from corn husks which cover the floors and ceilings to keep out drafts. These structures are architecturally superior to those found in Central Anatolia, and their basic design is similar to that of homes in Laz and other Georgian villages along the Black Sea Coast (see Ozgüner 1970).[1]

Traditionally, all building materials came from local sources and villagers displayed a great deal of self-sufficiency in construction. They cut trees from their own land, hauled them to the village mill to be sawed into posts and boards, and then hauled them to the building site. They prefer chestnut (a hard wood) for posts and poplar (a soft wood) for the lattice work on the roof upon which tiles rest. Formerly they could purchase red tile in the village from a family that produced it, but since the mid-sixties they have had to import it from either Inegöl or Bursa. Commonly, all members of the family and many neighbors worked side by side with a village builder hired to perform the more skillful operations and direct the building project. All those who worked, including the hired help, ate morning and noon meals with the building family.

Just outside a house's main door is a small cement platform on which villagers remove their outdoor footwear and step into clean wooden clogs or plastic slippers before entering. In most dwellings the entrance door opens directly into a large hall or anteroom (*sofa*) to which two, three, or four other rooms are connected. The first floor contains the kitchen, a general sitting room (*hayat*), and one or more bedrooms. The second floor resembles the first. Stairs lead up to its sitting room, which is adorned with glass windows that can be opened and divans built into two of its walls. Villagers use this space primarily in the summer as a family and guest room. They generally assign second story bedrooms to their adult offspring and/or married sons and their spouses.

In 1961 Hayriye homes had neither plumbing nor electricity. Women secured water in copper and earthenware jugs daily from the village's eight neighborhood fountains, and the sun illuminated homes during the day via their six to eight glass windows, while kerosene lamps provided faint halos of light at night. During subsequent years some villagers had water piped to their homes from nearby fountains, and in 1973 practically all homes got electricity. Most homes have separate toilets—crudely constructed wooden sheds placed above a trench. Some of the wealthier villagers have built

Fig. 10   Storing winter hay

Fig. 11   A Hayriye village home

privies attached to the second story of their homes, but the human waste merely falls to a pit below through the hollow of an old tree trunk.

Homes commonly contain simple wooden chairs, tables, chests, and cabinets that are either constructed locally by village carpenters or purchased in Inegöl. Some bedrooms contain bedsteads and mattresses, others only matresses that are rolled up and stored in cabinets during the day. Decorative items include colorful kilims (purchased outside Hayriye) covering the rush mats on the floors and manufactured printed cloth of nonindigenous design used for curtains and divan cushion covers. Villagers generally whitewash house interiors about twice a year, usually before holidays, and repair exteriors, which wear easily with wind and rain, every two or three years. The women of a household bake bread in an outdoor oven and prepare meals indoors over wood fires in a hearth or sheet-metal stove, which also provide heat in winter. Unlike Central Anatolian Turks, Hayriye villagers do not use dung in their home fires; they reserve it for field fertilizer.

Complementing the house are a two-story stable, a straw shed, a granary, and a unique elevated corn shed called a *bagen* (see Figure 2). The first three are commonly constructed of boards and may have tile roofs. The *bagen* is constructed of boards or timbers (both of horn beech) and set on top of four posts to expose it to air currents and prevent animals from climbing into its one or two rooms containing corn. The louvered sides and floor facilitate cross-ventilation which is necessary for the corn-drying process. All these buildings commonly face a courtyard enclosed by a high picket fence, which is as characteristic of Georgian villages as is the architecture of the house and *bagen*.

Every family does not own all the buildings comprising a complete and ideal homestead. In 1961 Hayriye contained 184 houses, 100 stables, 99 straw sheds, 69 *bagen*s, and 41 granaries. Those households lacking one or more of the auxiliary buildings had to compensate by increasing the functions of existing structures. As expected, households ranking highest on the village tax (*salma*) list (a list based on the property wealth of each household as estimated by the village chief and Council of Elders) possessed more buildings than others. Table 3 shows the average distribution of building types by household tax status.

Every village household owns its own home; the only renters in Hayriye are several teachers and forestry officials who have been assigned to the village. Those few households in the first three tax categories that possess more than one house either rent it out or assign it to a married son who remains an integral part of the extended family. According to Table 3 granary ownership has the clearest association with tax status. All eight households in the first tax category own a granary, as compared to only one of the 33 households ranked last.

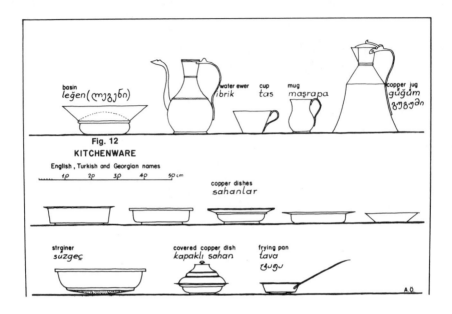

Fig. 12

KITCHENWARE

English , Turkish and Georgian names

basin
leğen (ოჯგენი)

water ewer
ibrik

cup
tas

mug
maşrapa

copper jug
güğüm
ბედედი

copper dishes
sahanlar

strainer
süzgeç

covered copper dish
kapaklı sahan

frying pan
tava
ცავა

A.Ö.

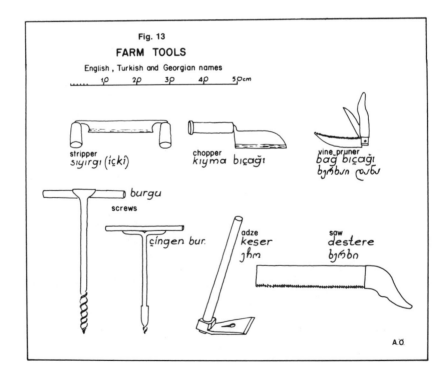

Fig. 13

FARM TOOLS

English , Turkish and Georgian names

stripper
sıyırgı (içki)

chopper
kıyma bıçağı

vine pruner
bağ bıçağı
ბაზან ცასა

burgu

screws

çingen bur.

adze
keser
ჯჩm

saw
destere
ბჯნბი

A.Ö.

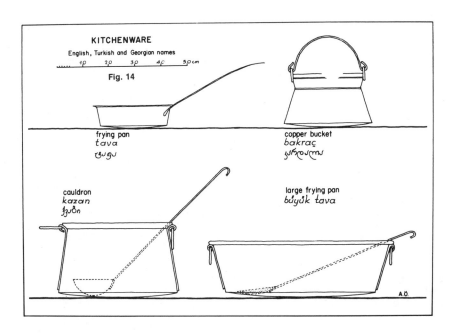

KITCHENWARE

English, Turkish and Georgian names

Fig. 14

frying pan
tava
ტაფა

copper bucket
bakraç
კარდალა

cauldron
kazan
ქვაბი

large frying pan
büyük tava

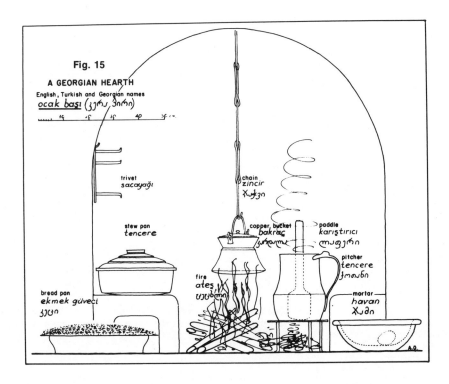

Fig. 15

A GEORGIAN HEARTH

English, Turkish and Georgian names

ocak başı (კერა, ბუხრი)

trivet
sacayağı

chain
zincir
ჯაჭვი

stew pan
tencere

copper bucket
bakraç
კარდალა

paddle
karıştırıcı
თაჯერი

pitcher
tencere
ჭურჭ̌ი

fire
ateş
ცეცხლი

bread pan
ekmek güveci
კეცი

mortar
havan
ჯამი

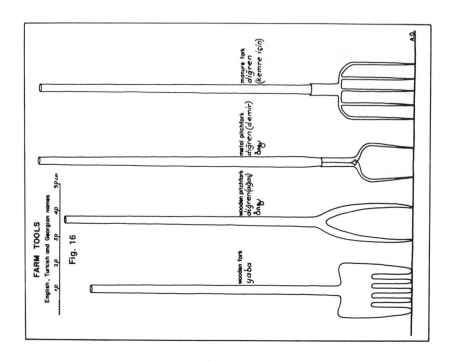

FARM TOOLS
English, Turkish and Georgian names

Fig. 16

wooden fork
yaba

wooden pitchfork
diğren(ağaç)
ǯyǯy

metal pitchfork
diğren(demir)
ǯyǯy

manure fork
diğren
(kemre için)

A.Ö.

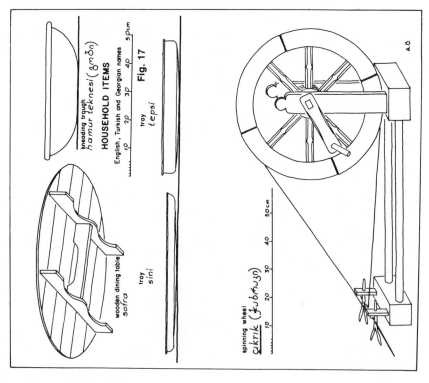

kneading trough
hamur teknesi (გობონ)

HOUSEHOLD ITEMS
English, Turkish and Georgian names

Fig. 17

tray
tepsi

wooden dining table
sofra

tray
sini

spinning wheel
çıkrık (ჩუბოჯგ)

A.Ö.

Table 3
Building Distribution by Tax Status of Households

Tax Status	Average Number of Buildings Owned				
	House	Bagen	Stable	Straw Shed	Granary
1	1.125	1.000	.875	.875	1.0
2	1.125	.750	.750	1.000	.50
3	1.060	.750	.900	.900	.48
4	1.000	.320	.680	.666	.15
5	1.000	.300	.630	.666	.12
6&7	1.000	.060	.280	.170	.03

Source: *Hayriye Köy Araştırma* 1963:92.

Land

In 1961 Hayriye's cultivated land totalled about 4,426 decares. (A decare or *dönüm* is equivalent to about 1/4 acre.) Table 4 shows the distribution of land by household tax status. Because a cadastral survey had not been conducted, ownership figures are approximations.

Table 4
Land Ownership by Household Tax Status
(in decares)

Tax Status	Total	Average	Index
1	668.0	83.50	100
2	429.5	47.77	57
3	1,029.5	34.19	41
4	1.024.5	25.63	26
5	888.0	17.37	21
6&7	339.5	12.73	12

Source: *Hayriye Köy Araştırma* 1963:36-37. (Corrected)

Three village households (all members of the first tax group) own more than 100 decares, the largest holding being 114 decares. Because inheritance practices tend to subdivide land each generation, most villagers work a number of plots ranging from one to five decares in size. Together, parcels of these sizes comprise 57% of Hayriye's cultivated land; six to ten decare plots comprise 28%; while 11 to 40 decare plots constitute the remaining 15%. The village's four largest plots are 40 decares (N=1), 30 decares (N=1), and 25 decares (N=2). Inheritance customs not only reduce the number of large plots, but actually decrease the amount of cultivated land because of the unplanted border strips created between parcels of different owners. When a large plot is subdivided, an estimated 1% of its total can be lost to borders; the corresponding figure for small parcels may be as great as 3% (*Hayriye Köy Araştırma* 1963:41).

As pointed out in the chapter on kinship and social organization, the size of households increases regularly with their wealth (as indexed by tax status) averaging only 3.2 members for households at the bottom of the tax scale and nine members for households at the top. In this chapter we will see that similar relationships exist between household wealth and land ownership, livestock ownership and productivity. Generally speaking, wealthier households have more members, own more land and livestock, and produce more per person than poorer households. These associations indicate the importance of a secure economic base for the establishment and maintenance of the ideal extended family.

Productivity and the triad of household size, land, and livestock are mutually influential. Obviously, the more land a household owns, the more it will produce and the more members it can support. However, two other relationships of equal importance may be less obvious. Productivity per decare depends in large part on a villager's ability to fertilize his land, and the main and almost exclusively used fertilizer in Hayriye is dung. Its availability depends on livestock, and livestock ownership corresponds to a household's ability to feed the animals through winter when they are stabled. Because winter fodder consists mostly of the by-products of agricultural produce, the number of decares and animals owned by a household are highly correlated. Hence, the factors of productivity per decare, household size, and the ownership of land and livestock are all closely related. The following pages will illustrate these relationships with actual and estimated figures.

Although all the agricultural land in Hayriye is owned and worked by village residents, traditionally there has not been enough for everyone. This has had a number of important socioeconomic consequences, one of which is the regular stream of emigration from the village to Inegöl and Bursa. Others have been the villagers' inability to fallow their land so that the organic matter content of the soil might increase, and the necessity of many of the village poor to labor for wages in the fields of the rich. In the early 1960s men earned from TL7 to TL10 a day for field work, while women only received TL5. In addition, about ten household heads worked approximately 200 decares of land on an *ortak* basis in the nearby villages of Konurlar and Maden. According to the *ortak* arrangement, landowners supply the land and half the seed, while users provide the other half of seed and all the labor. They divide the harvest equally.

Because much of the village is situated on slopes, erosion occasionally reduces crop yields of many plots drastically. Of the three common methods of preventing erosion—contour tillage, terracing, and strip cropping—Hayriye villagers employ only the first. Insufficient land and uncertain yields over the years had caused about half of the village's households to fall into debt by 1961. In addition to borrowing the maximum TL1,000 (about $111) at 7% from the government-financed Agricultural Cooperative, many had to seek money privately at annual rates of 10% to 20% (*Hayriye Köy Araştırma* 1963:63).

Land Use

The village's agricultural economy is very similar to the "traditional Georgian economy" described by Geiger *et al.* (1956:516-21). Hayriye's most significant exception is the absence of pigs, which were raised in Georgia by Georgian Christians free from the Muslim prohibition against eating pork. In Hayriye peasants have been at the mercy of the sun, wind, rain, hail, frost, and snow. They lack modern, scientifically developed high yield and disease-resistant strains of plants and animals as well as modern chemical fertilizers, herbicides, insecticides, and livestock medicines. Consequently, their yields fluctuate from year to year as fortune dictates.

They are plow agriculturalists involved in a close symbiotic relationship with their plants and animals, which together provide them with food, energy, fertilizer, cash, and some of their clothing. Draft animals have an especially close affinity to the soil. With their brawn they cultivate the earth and haul away its yield, and with their hooves they thresh its grains. They consume the stalks and leafy remains of crops, and in return fertilize the fields with their dung.

Because most villagers work small amounts of land, their dominant consideration when choosing crops is home consumption needs. Wealthy villagers with extensive land holdings enjoy the added luxury of contemplating sales in the Inegöl market. Table 5 lists most of Hayriye's major crops and the amounts of land devoted to each in 1961.

Corn. Corn, a New World plant, diffused to Europe through Spain after

Table 5
1961 Land Use Distribution

Crops	Decares	Per Cent
Chestnut trees	330.5	7.5
Apple Orchards	349.5	7.9
Pulses	227.5	5.1
Wheat	1,532.0	34.6
Corn	1,363.5	30.8
Tobacco	154.5	3.5
Other	468.5	10.6
Totals	4,426.0	100.0

Source: *Hayriye Köy Araştırma* 1963:41 (Corrected)

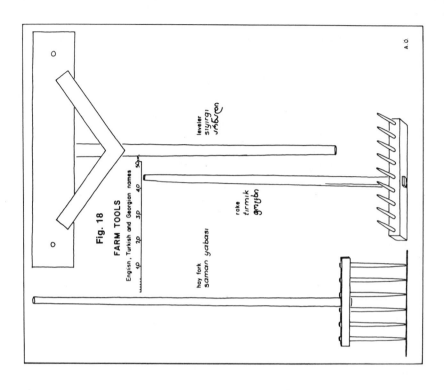

Fig. 18

FARM TOOLS

English, Turkish and Georgian names

leveler
sıyırgı
ჯაბურია

rake
tırmık
გოჯობი

hay fork
saman yabası

A.O.

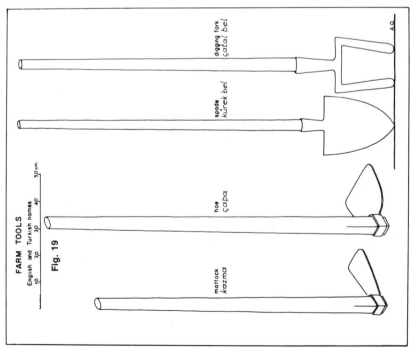

FARM TOOLS

English and Turkish names

Fig. 19

digging fork
çatal bel

spade
kürek bel

hoe
çapa

mattock
kazma

A.O.

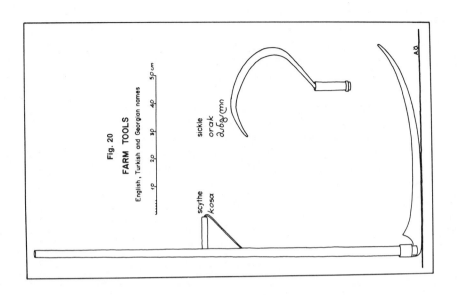

Fig. 20

FARM TOOLS

English, Turkish and Georgian names

scythe
kosa

sickle
orak
მანგალი

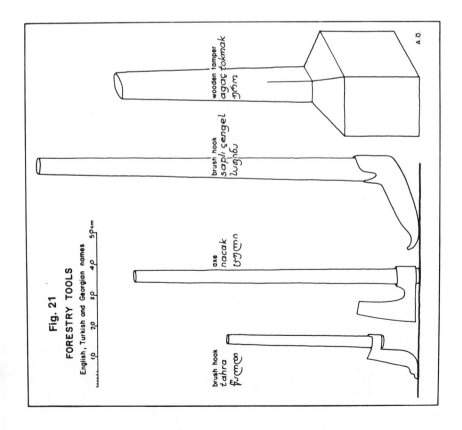

Fig. 21

FORESTRY TOOLS

English, Turkish and Georgian names

brush hook
tahra
ცული

axe
nacak
ცული

brush hook
sapli çengel
სატეხი

wooden tamper
agaç tokmak
ურო

Columbus' second voyage (1494) and then spread throughout Asia and Africa. It eventually became a staple food of peasants in Western Georgia, and Hayriye's settlers planted it soon after their arrival. People in the Inegöl Subprovince refer to it as "Georgian corn", and of the area villages only Hacıkara with its more fertile soil produces a higher quality yield.

All Hayriye households grow corn. They plow the fields first in March and then again in April or May to create furrows and sow seed (see Figure 25). They how in May or June and again in July and harvest in September. Families hand-pick, husk, and store the corn in their *bagens* where it dries. There they beat it with a mallet (*tokuezi*) causing the kernels to separate from the cobs and fall through the floor openings onto a clean spread or plastic sheet. Villagers store the corn in their granaries or houses and take it to the mill to be ground as needed.

Villagers measure corn by the *kile* (which for corn is approximately a bushel or 28 kilograms) and calculate a decare's yield at between 2.5 and five bushels a year. The total corn yield for 1961 was estimated at 126.7 tons. Although all households grow corn, all but the wealthiest consume their entire crop. Households in the first tax group sold an estimated 180 bushels in 1961 earning approximately TL3,150. Villagers occasionally eat corn roasted, but most often consume it in the form of a delicious, heavy bread called *jadi*. They also find the by-products of corn useful. Stalks and husks constitute winter feed for livestock and cobs provide fuel for home fires.

Table 6 shows the average corn yields by decare and household tax status. Households in the top brackets not only own more land, but produce larger yields per decare. This can be partly attributed to their greater ability to fertilize their plots (they own more livestock), some of which may be of higher quality to begin with.

Table 6
Average Corn Yields by Decare and Household Tax Status

Tax Status	Average no. of bu. per decare	Average no. of bu. per household
1	4.9	107.5
2	3.7	57.5
3	3.7	36.3
4	2.8	24.9
5	2.8	15.1
6&7	2.5	4.8

Source: *Hayriye Köy Araştırma* 1963:45.

Wheat and other grains. Wheat, like corn, is a major bread crop in Hayriye and has been planted here since the time of settlement. Villagers treat the two like sister crops by rotating them annually in the same plots. One year they plant corn on the east side of the river and wheat on the west; the next year they all switch directions. This rotation is a coordinated movement by which Hayriye peasants mark annual cycles in unison.

Most villagers plant wheat in October. (The Turkish word for October— *Ekim*—also means sowing.) Most work the land with a wooden plow (*saban*) pulled by a pair of oxen or water buffalo.[2] Both the plow and the manageable, slow moving animals are ideally suited for the rocky soil and sloping terrain. Some villagers use the heavier steel plow (*pulluk*) in the alluvial soils close to the river. The plowing season is relatively short as the wooden plows cannot penetrate the earth easily before the first autumn rains, and sowing must be completed in sufficient time to enable seedlings to take root before the initial frost.

Villagers harvest their wheat in August, reaping it by hand with sickles and scythes. They gather it together in bundles (sing. *demet*) and haul them to the threshing area in their wagons. There, they pile the bundles next to the threshing floor—a hard-stamped, sun-baked, circular platform of earth. They spread the bundles onto the floor a few at a time and drive the oxen-drawn *düven* ("traditional threshing sledge") over them so that the sharp flints on the underside of the sledge loosen the grain from the husk. They winnow by tossing the wheat into the air with a wooden fork (*yaba*), permitting the wind to blow the chaff to the side as the grain drops directly below. They then sift the wheat with a *kalbur* ("rimmed sieve with coarse mesh"), collect it into goat-hair sacks, and haul it to their granaries.

Threshing is a long process often requiring several weeks' labor. It takes a full day of hard work for several persons to thresh 50 bundles of wheat. By the early 1970s most villagers had decided to avoid this toil and manpower expenditure by contracting threshing machine operators outside Hayriye. In August, 1972 two machines were operating in the village, each threshing wheat at the rate of 50 bundles an hour for a charge of TL35.

Villagers grind most of their grain into flour for baking, but they try to save enough for the next season's planting. They use the by-product of wheat, straw, as winter fodder. Hayriye's average yield per decare of approximately three bushels (or 100.34 kilos) totalled about 152 tons in 1961.[3] Of this, households in the top tax bracket sold about 180 bushels. Hayriye villagers also plant small quantities of rye, barley, and oats for their own consumption needs. Table 7 shows average wheat production by household tax status.

Vegetables. Most village women cultivate kitchen gardens close to their homes which contain cucumbers, tomatoes, squash, carrots, pulses, lettuce, cabbage,

Fig. 22   Threshing grain

Fig. 23   Baking *pide*

Table 7
Average Wheat Production by Household Tax Status

Tax Status	Ave. decares planted	Ave. production by hh. (kilos)
1	30.0	115.6
2	17.6	61.3
3	12.4	42.3
4	8.6	26.6
5	5.3	18.1
6&7	2.7	10.1

Source: *Hayriye Köy Araştırma* 1963:48.

onions, peppers, and eggplant. Some men and women also grow tomatoes, cabbage, leeks, and squash among the corn and plant small plots of potatoes. Those fortunate enough to own some of the 227 decares along the river sow string beans there so they can water the plants easily. Villagers eat practically all of the vegetables they grow.

Fruits and nuts. During the 1950's apple production and sales became an important source of cash income for many village households and the situation has remained the same ever since. In 1961 the village had an estimated 3,200 apple trees, many of which were still in the sapling stage. As with many other items, the distribution of tree ownership varied regularly with household tax status. Most households in the fourth to seventh brackets owned fifteen trees or less, while those in the third to first brackets possessed thirty or more. Family members pick apples in the fall, bag them without regard to size or quality, and then either sell them to consumers in Inegöl or to middlemen who come to the village with their own trucks.

Villagers also sell limited quantities of pears and cherries. They experimented with growing strawberries commercially, but were dissatisfied with the results. Although plum and mulberry trees are abundant, villagers use their fruit for local consumption only.

Chestnuts may represent the village's most important cash crop. An elderly villager told me that one day several years after the Georgians had settled Hayriye, his father was clearing chestnut trees from a field when one of the many Armenians who lived in the area prior to World War I stopped him. After politely admonishing the Georgian for cutting down the valuable trees, he demonstrated how saplings could be grafted to mature trunks to produce exceptionally large chestnuts. All the villagers eventually adopted this new technology to their benefit, and in 1961 the village had approximately 2,000 chestnut trees spread over 330.5 decares. Depending on its size and age, a tree yields 20 to 100 kilograms of chestnuts annually. They sold for TL4.5/kg. in 1972. Average ownership by individual households ranged from seven trees for the poorest households to 33 for the richest ones.

Villagers also cultivate walnut and hazelnut trees for local consumption and limited external sales.

Tobacco and sunflower seed. In 1946 village chief Sabri Ertan's successful experiment with tobacco planting encouraged other villagers to engage in its production. Since then it has become an important cash crop. Villagers plow and prepare their tobacco fields in March, plant them with seedlings in late April, and hoe them in May and June. They pick tobacco from July to November, hang the leaves on the side of their stables or homes to dry, and prepare them for sale to the government, which maintains a monopoly on Turkish tobacco products. In 1961 average production per household ranged from 22.6 kilograms for the poorest households to 235 kilograms for the richest. Although tobacco production brings in needed cash, its labor demands are considerable, generally requiring all household members to contribute time and energy to the enterprise. As it would be unprofitable to hire help for this work, households with few members cannot engage in extensive production even if they have sufficient land.

Villagers began experimenting with sunflowers, another New World product, in the early 1950s and felt satisfied that the plant proved appropriate for Hayriye's soil and weather conditions. In 1961 they devoted about 75 decares to sunflowers and produced an average of ten bushels of seed per decare (one bu. of sunflower seed weighs 16 kg.) for a total yield of about 750 bushels. Villagers plow, sow, and hoe the fields at about the same times as they do for corn, and harvest in August when the backs of the sunflower heads become yellow and the outer bracts begin to turn down. They separate the seeds by beating the heads, which they feed to their cows in winter. Villagers eat some of the seed either raw or roasted, but take the bulk of it to the nearby village of Muratbey where they have it processed into oil. As payment for this service, they use the residue oil cake, which constitutes excellent livestock fodder.

Livestock

Livestock constitute an essential element in the peasants' scheme of survival. Hayriye is blessed with abundant pasturage; about 2,000 decares in or near the village and another 11,000 decares in the mountains. Two of the Yürük men in the village plus a few Georgians, who own little land, work as shepherds, driving flocks of sheep, goats, and cattle to increasingly higher elevation through the summer and then returning them in the fall. The villagers, whose animals they graze, pay them with corn and wheat.

Because this pasturage is common land, involving no rental expense to

Fig. 24   To the fields

Fig. 25   Plowing and Planting

its users, the size of herds in Hayriye is not determined by grazing costs, but by the ability of each household to feed its animals in the winter when they are stabled. Because winter fodder consists largely of the by-products of agricultural produce—corn stalks and husks, straw from grains, string bean plants, pea pods, and sunflower heads—animal and land ownership are closely related.

In 1961 Hayriye's 178 households owned 770 goats, 269 sheep, 129 donkeys, a few horses, and 563 head of cattle (145 oxen, 176 cows, 178 calves, 15 male water buffalo, 32 female water buffalo, and 17 water buffalo calves). All were local varieties. Table 8 shows the average numbers of livestock owned by households in the various tax categories.

Cattle. Villagers keep oxen and male water buffalo for drafting and cows for milk, from which they make yogurt, cheese, and butter. A cow averages one kilogram of milk daily and drops a calf once every two or more years. Cattle are slaughtered only when they become too old for their primary function. On those occasions, the villagers may keep some meat, give some to close kin, and sell most to other villagers. Or they might take the bulk of it to an Inegöl butcher who will convert it into sausage links which can be preserved up to a year. Lacking refrigeration, this is one of the few ways villagers can keep meat.

Sheep and goats. Of the various kinds of livestock raised in Hayriye, sheep may provide the greatest return on investment. Villagers shear them in July and November and use their wool to make socks, to stuff mattresses, pillows, cushions, and quilts, and for cash sales in Inegöl. In summer village girls rise early in the morning and walk through the dark up to the low pastures to milk the sheep, goats, and cows before the shepherds drive them to higher elevations for grazing. They generally get a half kilogram of milk daily from each ewe. In terms of butterfat content, villagers rate sheep milk first, water buffalo milk second, cow milk third, and goat's milk last. They frequently mix the first three

Table 8
Average Livestock Ownership by Household Tax Status

Tax Status	Cattle	Sheep	Goats	Donkeys
1	8.75	16.2	5.8	1.25
2	6.00	12.9	.9	.75
3	4.75	5.8	1.6	.82
4	3.46	3.6	1.9	.72
5	2.17	2.2	1.8	.78
6&7	.91	2.3	.5	.48

Source: *Hayriye Köy Araştırma* 1963:66,68,69. (Corrected)

to make butter, yogurt, and cheese. In addition, villagers enjoy a ready market for their rams, as mutton is one of Turkey's favorite meats. Wealthy villagers commonly slaughter one of their own rams on *Kurban Bayram* ("Islamic Feast of Sacrifice") and give much of the meat to Hayriye's poor.

Villagers raise goats for their milk, meat, and hair. They shear them once a year in June and sell most of the hair in Inegöl. Hayriye villagers use goat's milk in cheese, but because they find the meat repugnant they sell most of their he-goats. Although a goat is valued much less than a sheep or a head of cattle, its redeeming quality is its ability to fend for itself. Even in some of the worst weather, goats forage and endure. Hence, they represent very little expense to villagers *in the short run*. In the long run, however, they cost the villagers dearly. Their destructive eating habits and their intractability have contributed greatly to the area's erosion problems and the levying of costly fines by the government on villagers whose goats have strayed into restricted portions of the forest.Consequently, in 1972, when there were approximately 140 goats in Hayriye, residents agreed to sell them all and prohibit their future ownership in the village.

Horses and donkeys. Although no one in Hayriye owned a motorized vehicle in 1961, truck and minibus transportation to Inegöl was provided almost daily by private entrepreneurs outside the village. During earlier decades Hayriye villagers had traveled by horse whenever they wished to go any distance. They considered riding donkeys shameful. With the availability of trucks and buses, however, horses became luxuries that only a few wealthy persons could comfortably afford, and Georgian men dropped their prohibition against riding donkeys. They began utilizing them (much as their Turkish neighbors always had) both for riding to and from their fields and for carrying light loads. Nevertheless Hayriye women have continued to observe the customary proscription and demonstrate, thereby, their greater propensity to preserve tradition. As Table 8 shows, most households (with the exception of those in the lowest tax group) own at least one donkey.

Poultry. Practically every household keeps a few to a dozen chickens both for their eggs and meat, which they can preserve for two or three months by salt curing. In recent years a small number of households have acquired a few ducks and turkeys, which like chickens roam and forage freely.

Bees and silk worms. At one time in the past a significant number of households engaged in honey and silk production, however since the late 1950s only a few have been so involved.

Other Economic Activities

Most Hayriye adults earn their livelihoods exclusively from agriculture. But some combine farming with other economic activities. Traditionally

Fig. 26 Preparing bean poles

several men have offered barber services to individuals on an annual contract basis. They shaved and cut hair either in a coffeehouse or in their customers' homes for a bushel of wheat a year. In the late 1950s one barber opened a small shop and began charging by the individual shave or haircut. Eventually, this mode of payment became standard.

Blacksmithing is provided by a father, his two sons, and another villager. They operate out of their own stables and charge a bushel of wheat to keep an animal in shoes for a year. One other family operates a small sawmill in which villagers have logs cut into boards for building purposes.

Several men, with help from their families, have operated small general stores selling needles, pins, hardware, biscuits, cologne, kerosene lamps, salt, toothpaste, and other miscellaneous items. They offer seasonal credit to relatives and trusted friends.

In 1957 the government's educational extension service opened a two year general building course in Hayriye. Twenty men enrolled the first year and fifteen the next. As a consequence, one villager became a qualified journeyman who constructs all types of buildings in Hayriye for wages, and two others left the village for the cities so that they could apply their newly acquired skills full-time. At different times carpentry courses have been similarly offered and a few of the men who attended now make household items, such as tables, chairs, and cabinets on order.

The forest has provided Hayriye villagers with an additional source of income. Originally they had free access to the trees, which they cleared from their fields or cut for building material and fuel. Then the government declared Ulu Mountain a national preserve and began strictly controlling the forest. Now villagers can earn extra money by either hauling logs with their oxen for the government or cutting wood and selling it to middlemen. The Forestry Office grants villagers permits for a small fee to cut wood in designated areas. However, the villagers complain that the formality of acquiring a permit is long and involved and that the designated cutting areas are usually inaccessible. Consequently, they cut wood without permission arguing that the forest was theirs to start with. Over the decades forest guards have arrested practically every Hayriye adult male at least once for violating forestry regulations. Convicted villagers generally lose their axes and receive fines. During the late 1950s and early 1960s approximately thirty village men worked an estimated fifty days a year for TL12 a day for the Forestry Office which was constructing a road into the forest.

Annual Work Cycle
The full details of the annual work cycle in Hayriye are so numerous that

a full inventory of them would be beyond our time and space limitations. Instead, we will discuss the cycle with reference to only a limited number of significant factors.

Figure 9 shows the monthly distribution of farm labor by women, men, and animals, which is devoted to the sowing, cultivation, and harvest of Hayriye's most important food and cash crops: corn, wheat, sunflower, apples, chestnuts, and tobacco. The graph offers two types of comparisons. The bars themselves show the relative amounts of farm work (devoted to the above six crops only) that women, men, and draft animals engage in each month. For example, in August men work about twice as much as women, while in June they labor almost equally. The three vertical scales on the left help the reader determine the proportion of annual farm labor expended by women, men, and draft animals in any given month. In August, for example, men expend about 33% of their total annual farm labor, as compared to 24% for women.

A very brief breakdown of monthly activities devoted to the six crops is as follows:

October: Men plow fields and plant winter wheat; women and children cure and strip tobacco.

October through January: Men, children, but especially women work on tobacco curing, stripping, and general preparation for market.

February: Villagers devote their time to other activities.

March through May: In March and April men plow and harrow fields in preparation for the May planting of corn, sunflower, and tobacco.

June and July: Men and women hoe fields.

August: Men and women harvest grains and employ draft animals to thresh wheat. Women and children begin picking tobacco and apples. (Note that in figure 9 the bar representing the amount of draft animal labor in the September column most likely has been misplaced and should belong in the August column instead.)

September: Men, women, and children complete the harvest of tobacco, corn, apples, and chestnuts.

Although numerous activities, such as the cultivation of kitchen gardens and the care of livestock, have been omitted, the above offers a fair representation of the tempo of agricultural activity in Hayriye. Villagers commonly say that they work hard when it is warm to feed their throats

Fig. 27   Cleaning silk cocoons

when it is cold. As winter approaches they must turn their attention to the preparation of their homestead. They close any cracks in the walls with mud plaster, shut windows tight, cover floor openings with plastic sheets and rush mats, finish collecting firewood and cut it to size, and set up winter stoves. During the winter men feed, water, and groom their livestock which are now stabled, and spend much of their free time in one of the coffeehouses with friends. Women continue their routine of preparing meals and baking bread, but frequently gather together with friends to weave rush mats, sew socks, or patch and repair clothes while engaging in conversation. Boys and girls spend a great deal of time with their sexually segregated peer groups.

For certain major activities, like sickling wheat and hoeing corn, members of four or five different households have traditionally formed collective work groups which.informally exchange labor. Such reciprocity, called *nadi* (Georg.) locally, corresponds to a general form of cooperation among relatives and friends that is found in many peasant societies. In lieu of paying wages, members of the host household serve the exchange work group breakfast and lunch and reciprocate by working in the fields of those who worked with them. The arrangement answers both economic and social needs. Participants provide each other with quality work and enjoyable companionship as they toil, converse, joke, and sing together in the fields.[4]

Gross Village Product

The 1961 METU study offers us information from which we can estimate what Hayriye's Gross Village Product (GVP) would be given its 1961 population and level of technology and favorable weather conditions. By GVP we mean the market value of agricultural and animal products, whether consumed locally or sold, plus any income earned from wages, services, etc. performed either inside or outside the village by its residents. Unfortunately, the METU study did not give full consideration to the costs of production and sale. Consequently, the resulting figures are higher than they would have been had such items as the cost of purchased seed, transportation, and loan interest been included in the computation. Table 9 breaks down the total estimated GVP of approximately $153,745 into its various categories.

Table 10 has been constructed on the assumption that the village's Total Agricultural Product (TAP) of TL 1,120,370 (about $124,485) would be distributed among village households in direct proportion to the amount of land owned by each, which is represented in the table by the household land ownership index. The resulting figures show that the average amount of TAP per individual in the eight wealthiest households is about $249 or almost triple the approximately $84 average per person in the 33 poorest households. The average TAP per person index systematically shows other differences.

Table 9
Hayriye's 1961 Gross Village Product
(Estimated in Turkish Lira)

Agricultural Product

Crops	782,940
Other land-use product	17,600
Animal products	319,830
Total Agricultural Product	1,120,370

Non-Agricultural Income

Forestry labor income	201,150
Work outside village	15,000
Village services	47,200
Total Non-Agricultural Income	263,350
Gross Village Product	1,383,720

Source: *Hayriye Köy Araştırma* 1963:111. (Corrected)

If we divided Hayriye's 1961 Gross Village Product (see Table 9) by the village's 910 inhabitants, the resulting figure of TL 1,520.6 (per. pers. GVP) could be usefully compared to several national income figures for 1960. In that year, Turkey's per capita national income was TL 3,414. Per capita Agricultural income was only TL 1,975.7, while per capita industrial income was TL 7,158.7 (Keleş 1972:15). Thus, it appears that Hayriye was poorer than average for agricultural villages, and that in Turkey generally a wide disparity existed between rural people and those in industrial, urban centers.

Conclusion

Hayriye's is a peasant economy with a labor-intensive technology in which agriculture predominates both in terms of labor and production. The basic units of production are households, composed of either nuclear or extended families. Most households are orientated first to their own sustenance and secondarily to external markets.

The agricultural work cycle has traditionally provided Hayriye with its tempo and rhythm. All villagers have had to organize their lives and

Table 10
1961 Total Agricultural Product (TAP)
(Estimated in Turkish Lira)
per Household and Person
by Tax Status and
Index of Land Ownership

Tax Status	No. of hhs	Ave. land ownership index	Ave. TAP per hh.	Ave. TAP per pers.	TAP per pers. index
1	8	100	20,200	2,244	100
2	9	57	11,514	1,619	72
3	30	41	8,282	1,342	60
4	47	26	5,252	987	44
5	51	21	4,242	924	41
6&7	33	12	2,424	760	34

Based on figures presented in *Hayriye Köy Araştırma* 1963.

arrange their plans with primary deference to the basic movements of agriculture's symphony: plowing, sowing, hoeing, and harvesting. Only when the final movement has been concluded could families marry their offspring, circumcise their sons, and engage in other social events whose scheduling must be subordinated to the time requisites of farming.

Hayriye's elected officials categorize households on the basis of their property wealth into seven tax statuses, but for purposes of socioeconomic analysis one could usefully rearrange the households into high, medium, and low wealth groups by combining tax statuses one with two, three with four, and five and six with seven. Although these three groups are not rigid social classes, generally speaking, households in different groups experience different living standards, receive differential respect, and support different political parties (see Chapter VI). For example, wealthy household heads commonly see themselves as village leaders with socioeconomic obligations to those less fortunate. They employ the poor, give them outright gifts of food and clothing (especially on Islamic holidays), make the largest contributions to public projects, grant the village the benefit of their wisdom and experience, and are the most likely to make the important pilgrimage to Mecca. In return they earn greater increments of respect and prestige.

The village poor represent the opposite extreme of the socioeconomic pole. They lack sufficient capital to support themselves and must either seek non-agricultural employment or labor for the rich who own more land than they can work themselves. Consequently, an alliance of economic necessity exists between many of the rich and poor. The medium wealth group's land and livestock are sufficient to make them economically independent of the rich, but inadequate to support a position of socio-economic prominence. Hence, they enjoy more prestige and deference than the poor, but less than the rich.

Despite these important social differences, which vary rather consistently with economic status, sharp cleavages between wealth groups do not exist. Intergroup cohesion is continuously promoted by a number of cultural forces, including an ideology of Muslim brotherhood, diffuse kinship ties, and a common identity with Hayriye as a unique village and Georgian community.

NOTES

1. For a discussion of home and village arrangements in Georgia, see Robakidzé (1963).

2. Hayriye's first two tractors were purchased by villagers in the late 1960s and early 1970s with money earned in Germany. Prior to these, there were no privately owned motorized vehicles in the village.

3. In 1970, Turkey's average yield per *dönüm* of wheat was 120 kilos. It rose to 150 kilos in 1975, which was substantially lower than the 190 kilos achieved in nearby Greece (*Quarterly Economic Review* 1976:6).

4. Grigolia (1939:172) offers a romantic description of this traditional custom of reciprocal help as it was found in Western Georgia:

> The cultivation of maize, which is the principal staple food in Western Georgia, requires much labor and care. The main work consists in weeding out the over-growth from the fields... To accomplish this work without any assistance on the part of the villagers would be impossible for a single family, and failure to do this meant the loss of the harvest and consequently privation and endangering of the very existence of the family. The way out of this difficult position is found in the custom of mutual assistance and the reciprocal help in the cultivation of the land, which is known under the Georgian name of *nadoba*.
>
> During the time of sowing or weeding out of the maize field, the Megrelian villager calls his neighbors for assistance and every one of them willingly goes to help him. The owner provides a good lunch and heavy supper, with plenty of wine. In the evening, when the day's work is over, they return from the field singing, and sit at the supper table for a long time, singing the national songs and making speeches until late in the night...

6
Politics
and Government

Because local politics and village administration have been strongly influenced and often determined by national developments, this chapter begins with a brief discussion of Turkey's recent political history and then moves to the village level.

National Politics

In 1923 the Turkish Republic found its initial footing among the crumbled foundations of the Ottoman Empire. The Republic's leader, Mustafa Kemal (later called Mustafa Kemal Ataturk) freed post-World War I Turkey from Greek and other foreign occupation and embarked on an ambitious plan to remold the country into a modern nation-state in the image of the leading European powers. This challenge required the creation of a new set of national symbols so that the different peoples of Turkey might shift their loyalties and identities away from the various components of the multinational, Islamic-Ottoman Empire of the past to the uninational, secular Republic of the future.

Islam's role as the pervasive symbol of collective identity had to be taken over by a national-legal abstraction called "Turkish citizenship," and the national identities of the country's many non-Turkish residents had to be denied so as to prevent potentially conflicting loyalties from splintering the new state's envisioned unity. To facilitate the creation of this Turkish national homeland official histories were written which "explained" that many of the country's minorities, such as the Kurds, Circassians, and Georgians, were basically Turks who spoke mutually unintelligible Turkish dialects. Such citizens would be pressured into learning true Turkish, and publications in their own languages were, and still are, prohibited.

Ataturk decreed that the new Turkey would be based on the principles of nationalism, secularism, statism, populism, and reformism (see Karpat 1959). Among his many revolutionary acts were numerous secular reforms: the abolition of the Caliphate and Sultanate, the disestablishment of Islam as the State religion, the closing of the religious schools and brotherhoods, the replacement of Islamic law with European codes, the abolition of the Faculty of Theology, the replacement of Arabic script with Latin letters, and the prohibition of the fez—the customary Muslim headgear.

From 1923 until his death in 1938, Kemal Ataturk ruled Turkey through a single party, the Republican People's Party (RPP), as a benevolent but firm dictator, who allowed no opposition to stand in the way of his reforms. Two experiments with multiparty politics "failed" when he quickly lost patience with opposition that he felt only impeded the country's rate of progress.

Ataturk's successor, Ismet Inonu, continued the secularist policies with equal vigor. For numerous reasons, including his desire to fulfill Ataturk's ultimate ambition to establish a Western democracy in Turkey, Inonu announced in 1945 that he would permit another experiment in multiparty politics. Dissident members of the RPP, who opposed the government's rigid stance on religion and the economy, immediately organized the Democrat Party (DP). This new party found support among businessmen disgruntled by strict wartime economic controls, consumers suffering from the high cost of living, Christians and Jews who had to pay a discriminatory tax (*varlık vergisi*) in 1942, elitist groups whose ambitions were not being promoted by the RPP, and millions of malcontent peasants who resented the RPP's neglect of agriculture and suppression of religious expression (Rustow 1957). In 1950, the first open and honest election of the Turkish Republic gave the DP a resounding victory, and the Republicans honored the people's will by stepping down. "Turkey thus became perhaps the only country in modern history in which an autocratic regime peacefully gave up the reins of government" (Tachau 1972:382).

The Democrats created an atmosphere of religious tolerance by allowing the Arabic call to prayer and including Islamic instruction in the regular primary school curriculum as a voluntary course. Religious expression, long forced to remain secret or dormant, asserted itself openly once again. Nevertheless, the DP accepted Ataturk's principles and acted against religious extremism.

The political divisions manifested during this era grew out of the country's dichotomous socioeconomic structure. The RPP rested on a supportive alliance of urban elite, civil bureaucrats, military leaders, and large landowners, who through their affiliation with the party were able to reenforce their domination over the peasantry, who together with the urban poor comprised about 75% to 80% of the country's population.

The DP, having found support among the disinherited and the RPP's own disenchanted, took a number of social and economic measures during its period of rule (1950-60) which altered this dichotomy. It gave more benefits to rural areas: roads, electric projects, farm credits, aid for building construction, new industry, more educational and medical facilities, and elimination of the dreaded road tax. These contributed to the villagers' new capacity for political awareness and involvement, and their greater integration with the country. In the cities, DP support for private industry and commerce facilitated the development of an urban elite that rivaled or surpassed the high bureaucratic and military echelons in terms of wealth and status. Turkish citizens who profited from the DP's socioeconomic measures and/or who valued the greater freedom of religious expression returned the party to power in 1954 and 1957. These events served to increase frustration and resentment among RPP supporters who were suffering from withdrawal of status.

To compensate for their impotence at the election polls, the frustrated urban supporters of the RPP began expressing their antigovernment sentiments in the press and through public demonstrations. In 1960, when the government increasingly relied on the army to quell the "illegal riots" of political protest by university students in Ankara and Istanbul, the military leadership decided that civilian politics had failed.

Headed by General Cemal Gursel, the military carried out a bloodless coup, arresting Democrats holding national office and replacing most Democrats in municipal offices with either military officers or RPP members. During the ensuing period of martial law, the military permanently outlawed the DP and purged its own officer ranks of DP sympathizers. Former DP Prime Minister Menderes was accused of violating the constitution, and after litigation he was condemned to death along with his Foreign and Finance Ministers. A new constitution was prepared, containing safeguards against political extremism and protecting Ataturk's reforms, "which aim at raising Turkish society to the level of contemporary civilization" (Article 153).

The junta returned the government to the politicians in 1961, and the country witnessed the birth of numerous parties that vied for the support of former Democrat voters. Eventually, most of the DP men who were allowed to reenter politics reorganized under the banner of the Justice Party (JP), which soon became heir to the DP. One political analyst has concluded that the JP's popularity and representativeness qualify it as the first truly grass-roots party in the Middle East (Sherwood 1967).

The RPP, hoping to win support among radicalizing elements of the urban intelligentsia, altered its political ideology in 1965 and moved "left-of-center." This new orientation alienated conservative elements among the general voting public, and the JP won electoral victories in 1965 and 1969.

Throughout much of the 1960s and into the 1970s deteriorating relations with the United States, largely stemming first from the Johnson administration's and then the U.S. Congress's handling of the Greco-Turkish conflict over Cyprus, facilitated the spread of anti-American/anti-NATO sentiments and the spread of left-wing radicalism in Turkey. Tensions between rightist and leftist groups frequently erupted into turbulent labor strikes, student riots, and urban violence. Despite its numerical superiority in the Grand National Assembly, the JP's inability to deal effectively with the political anarchy prompted the Turkish military chiefs to stage a "coup by communique" in March 1971, which called for the resignation of the JP government and the formation of a nonpartisan coalition. Martial law was declared in eleven provinces; real power was once again in the hands of the military.

The following several years witnessed a series of ineffectual "above party" or caretaker governments. As a result of new elections in 1973, the left-of-center RPP emerged as the largest party in Parliament, although no party had a majority. In 1974 Ecevit formed an unlikely coalition with the right-wing National Salvation Party and experienced a short period of glory when Turkish Forces invaded Cyprus to protect the Turkish minority there and gained control of 40% of the island. Ecevit's government, however, soon proved unworkable, and he resigned in September of the same year.

After another ineffectual caretaker government, the resilient Suleyman Demirel, leader of the JP and premier from 1965 to 1971, put together a right-of-center "national front" coalition which won a narrow vote of confidence (222 to 218) in April, 1975. Clashes between the right and left as well as student violence continue unabated, and the 1977 general elections resulted in yet another weak coalition government headed by Demirel.

The founders of the Turkish Republic planned to bring the country to a state of Western democracy through the authoritarian rule of a single party, but their long period of unrivaled political control set a contradictory precedent. Subsequent multi-party politics became the kind of zero-sum game played by leaders of many new African states in which a win-all or lose-all attitude prevails (see W.A. Lewis 1965). While occupying the seat of power both the RPP and the DP resorted to extreme measures to maintain their positions. The political system's corrective mechanism has been the military, rather than the voting booth (Magnarella 1974:135). For much of the past decade, Turkey has been seeking an elusive stability. Currently, the country appears to be on the threshold of a major political transition.

Local Government: History and Developments

It appears that village government in Turkey evolved from an old, indigenous system whereby the male heads of lineages within a settlement gathered together periodically to discuss matters of mutual concern. If one or a few lineages dominated economically, their leaders made the important decisions, otherwise all men participated in a more or less democratic way. Probably, it was common for a village elder who had earned special prestige for his wisdom, fairness, and wealth to become regarded as the village's headman (*muhtar*, an Arabic term). " This system seems to have been compatible with the 'superficial' nature of Ottoman rule which seemed generally satisfied with governing a multitude of autonomous groups (including villages, guilds, nomadic tribes and ethnic groups) via a local leader responsible for maintaining order and collecting taxes..." (Scott 1968:16). Under these circumstances, villagers were, for the most part, internally oriented, and the headman could work for the good of his village and earn additional increments of local prestige. This situation changed markedly during the early Republican period with the introduction of the 1924 Village Law.

Ataturk's envisioned transformation of the Turkish mentality could only be accomplished if the largest segment of the population, the peasantry, was absorbed into his ideological cause. Given the country's dual problems of limited resources and widely scattered rural population, the reformers hoped that sociocultural and economic change among the peasants could be achieved through legislation—specifically through the Village Law of 1924 which formalized acceptable aspects of tradition while decreeing elements of the envisioned future.

The law defined a village as a settlement with a population of less than 2,000, and gave such a settlement the status of a legal or juridical person. Comprising the villagers' new life plan were lists of 37 compulsory duties and 31 voluntary ones. On the compulsory agenda were such items as eliminating stagnant water pools within village boundaries, because they promote mosquitoes that cause malaria; surrounding the mouths of village wells with stones to a height of 27 inches; separating the stable and living sections of each home by a wall; constructing two roads to run the length and breadth of the village, crisscrossing it in the center; planting a minimum of one tree a year per man between the village and its cemetery, along streams and roads, and in the central square; not causing animals to be overloaded or tired needlessly; killing insects and birds, which damage crops, according to procedures specified by the government; maintaining village roads; constructing a school with a garden in the most desirable part of the village in accordance with government directions; constructing a village meeting room and guest room; constructing village wagon, grocery, and blacksmith shops; and building private privies for every village home and a general one for the village (Sections 12,13).[1]

The optional list advised villagers to whitewash the outside walls of their homes, privies, and stables once a year; construct a village laundry, bath, and market place; purchase machines to make cheese and butter; collectively construct irrigation ditches for fields and gardens; purchase manufactured fertilizers for greater yields and books for more knowledge; organize village sports; purchase thoroughbred rams, he-goats, stallions, and bulls; aid the village poor with food and money; have orphans circumcised; help girls marry; and provide shrouds for the corpses of the poor (Section 14).

Despite the fine intentions of the idealistic lawmakers, sociocultural and economic development is not the fruit of decree; it requires adequate natural and human resources, organization, finances, and effective communication links. Unfortunately, the villagers were uneducated, remote, and poor. Hence, the law's social and economic innovations existed as unenforceable, paper models, and the vast majority of villagers continued to live outside the mainstream of the Kemalist revolution. Richard D. Robinson, an American who studied the rural Turkish scene in the late 1940s, offers some insightful conclusions about the Village Law and peasant life.

> The Village Law is all too often buried in oblivion. Inadequate funds, the absence of many literate leaders in the villages, and the lack of village initiative are all cited as contributing causes. For my part, I would tend to place a good share of the blame on the psychology of the government which wrote the law. For instance, not only does the law enumerate those duties required of a village (under threat of punishment), but also those things which a village may do if it wishes. If anything not specifically delegated to the village is proposed, permission must first be secured from the Central Government—in many cases, from Ankara. Such a law leaves little room for individual

> or village responsibility and rights. What is given by the Central Government can just as easily be taken away by it. The situation is exactly the reverse of that existing in the United States where all power and authority not expressly delegated to a higher unit of government—be it city, county, state, or national—remains with the lower unit and, basically, with the individual. The latter system breeds responsibility; the former, disinterest [Robinson 1949].

Although the Village Law did not affect living standards and lifestyles, it did formalize village administration. According to the Law all members of a village who have reached 21 years of age comprise the Village Assembly, which should meet every four years to select a headman and Council of Elders (*Ihtiyar Heyeti*). (In only a small percentage of villages do women actually attend these meetings and vote.) The Council's size should be eight members for villages under 1,000 population, and twelve members for larger villages. In an apparent effort to broaden representation, the Law grants the village's *imam* ("prayer leader") and secular teacher with *ex officio* membership, while it prohibits close relatives from serving on the Council simultaneously. The Council is supposed to meet weekly to decide village policy and advise the headman. Among its specific duties are setting the amount of local tax (*salma*) for each household, deciding which projects should be undertaken with communal labor (*imece*), and settling local disputes.

The Village Law makes the headman the highest elected official of the village and the local representative of the national government. Listed for him are 16 obligations to the state and 7 to his village. This differential evinces the Republican lawmakers' intention to convert this traditionally internally oriented role into an externally oriented one that would be subservient to the state. The traditional village leader was to become a state functionary, although his small salary is paid by his fellow villagers.

The headman's state duties include: informing the authorities of folk healers and preventing them from treating the village ill; vaccinating villagers against contagious diseases; registering village births, deaths, marriages, and divorces monthly; aiding the state tax collector; assembling village daftees and reporting deserters or draft-dodgers; aiding the gendarmes and the court's process-servers; as well as announcing, explaining, and executing laws and regulations proclaimed by the government. His most important village duties are collecting and spending local taxes, commencing communal work projects, and investigating local disputes in consultation with the Council of Elders (Sections 35,36,37).

The actual operation of village government depends on numerous factors which vary from settlement to settlement, such as existing economic relations, kinship ties, and alliances among significant social groups. In some villages the Councils are inactive and the headman operates alone, in others they work together.

Additional changes during the early Republican period increased the headman's reorientation from his village to the state, more specifically to the single party of the state: the RPP. At the 1927 RPP convention it was decided that all village headmen had to be approved by RPP inspectors before assuming office. The Party and state administrations were merged further in 1935 when the Minister of Interior was made the Party's General Secretary and the provincial governors were appointed chairmen of the local party organizations (Payaslioğlu 1964:421). During the single party rule of the RPP (1923-46) governmental authoritarianism reigned supreme. Directives flowed one way: from the top to bottom, capital to village. The intelligentsia and urbanites, imbedded in their traditional postures of superiority, provided no channel for rural feedback (Karpat 1973:276).

Given this structure, a common type of headman was the traditional-paternalistic *ağa*, a large landowner and head of a dominant lineage. He generally entered into an alliance or "understanding" with the RPP, whereby he kept his villagers in line and carried out "essential"government directives in return for the preservation of his own dominant position and the backing of the rural gendarmes. Those village *ağa*s who wanted to enjoy the fruits of this arrangement while avoiding the headaches of the post put up weak headmen, whom they controlled.

In any case, a headman who faithfully tried to perform his duty as defined by law would be extremely unpopular with his fellow villagers and would have no time left for his own work. Hence, in many villages, especially in those lacking *ağa*s, the headmanship became an undesirable chore and the most able and respected villagers would not take it.

During the multiparty period, especially from 1950 to 1960, the alliance between the RPP and the local *ağa*s was largely ended. In most settlements the poorer villagers, who are always in the majority, flocked to the Democratic Party and elected headmen of their own. Internal village factions took on political labels as different groups openly supported candidates of various parties for the position. Concomitant with this change was an opening up of the communication process. The Democrats were interested in what the villagers had to say, because the large village vote kept them in office.

The National Unity Committee, which governed Turkey after the 1960 military coup that threw the Democrats out of office, tried unsuccessfully to reduce village factionalism by prohibiting political parties from both organizing on the village level and putting up candidates for village offices. The Committee believed that political party rivalry in villages leads to their disruption, because political discussion is not possible in places where the most basic needs have not been met (Dodd 1969:133). The decree later became part of the Village Law (as revised in 1963) and the Political Parties' Law of 1965. But despite this legislation, local party leaders resumed their roles as rural organizers and party communication channels when the military turned the government back over to the political parties in 1961 (Karpat 1973:278-79), and in the minds of most villagers, the candidates for headman still run as members of distinct political parties.

The trend to integrate the villages into national life through active governmental attention and national investment as initiated by the Democratic Party continued after the 1960 revolution in a somewhat more organized fashion. For example, the State Planning Organization established a Community Development section which began a series of pilot projects in selected subprovinces (*ilçler*) to instruct government officials and village leaders in the concepts, organization, and goals of regional and community development. A new Ministry of Village Affairs was created to consolidate and coordinate the numerous village-level projects that other ministries had initiated, and the Ministry of Education accelerated its village school building program, while the Ministry of Health established an Academy of Social Work with a focus on village problems (Scott 1968:26-28).

In addition to a number of case studies describing the variety of headmen in Turkish villages (e.g., Scott 1968; Stirling 1965; Szyliowicz 1966; Kolars 1963; Yasa 1955), there have been two national village surveys which offer useful statistical information. The first of these surveys (sponsored by the Turkish State Planning Organization and U.S. Agency for International Development and conducted in 1962 under the direction of Frederick W. Frey) consists of interview data collected from approximately 8,000 persons living in 446 villages scattered across all 67 Turkish provinces. A number of generalizations about headmen resulting from this survey are as follows: 1) Headmen tended to be more literate[2] and affluent than the average villager. 2) About three-quarters of the respondents designated the headman as the most "influential" person in their village, and the major reason given for this influence was the headman's official position. 3) The more isolated a village (as measured in terms of distance from the nearest, well-traveled road), the more influential did its residents regard their headman. 4) However, the presence of an *ağa* in the village notably weakened the headman's position in the eyes of his fellow villagers (Frey and Roos 1967).

The second survey (sponsored by the Turkish State Planning Organization and conducted in 1968) contains interview data collected from a representative national sample of 5,244 persons living in 220 villages. These data permit us to draw the following generalizations about village headmen: 1) About 93% of the headmen claimed they could read and write in the new alphabet[3] as compared with similar claims made by 61.8% of the other adult village males interviewed. 2) Approximately two-thirds of the respondents named the headman as the most influential person in their village. The regional breakdown of this response was 70.5% for the "developed" provinces of the West; 66.9% for the "semi-developed" provinces of the North, South, and Center; and only 54.1% for the "less developed" provinces of the East in which village *ağa*s are most predominant. The major reasons given for the headman's influence were his "official position" (29.3%) and his "intelligence-initiative" (28.1%). 3) The smaller the village (and probably the more remote), the more likely was its headman to be named the most influential person in it. 4) The headman and members of the Council of Elders were most frequently mentioned as the persons most often consulted in cases of trouble (64.1%) (*Modernization in Turkish Villages* 1974).

Studies conducted to date provide us with two basic hypotheses about the relationship between the headman and other important socio-economic and political variables. The first hypothesis, a rather dogmatic and static one, was put forth by the Turkish social scientist Kiray (1968:113) in a chapter entitled: "Some Notes on Elected Headmen and Mayors in Different Communities of Turkey." She writes as follows:

> Our observations in extensive field studies...show that the question of who will be elected in any community is always determined by the balance amongst the different powers of that community. In our type of society where the basic feudal social structure still prevails, the elected local administrative authorities always belong to and serve in the continuation of this structure and maintain the status-quo...

The second hypothesis is more dynamic in that it focuses on change, especially in the relationship between modernization and the village headmanship. Although not strictly stated in the form of a hypothesis, Frey's writing based on his analysis of the 1962 village survey data represents an early statement of this position:

> Our personal impression is that the overall position and characteristics of the *muhtar* indicate that he might well be utilized as the focal figure in the modernization of Turkish villages. He is clearly an individual of formidable power and authority. He plays a central role between the village and outside agencies as well as in the internal communications structure of the village. He would seem generally to be more interested in and responsive to modernization than most male villagers...He seems definitely to be of the group, an accepted member of peasant society.... There are many signs in this survey that a program of *muhtar* re-education and training might well be the most economical and effective way to further the rapid development of rural Turkey [Frey as quoted in Stycos 1965:130].

In his study of the Turkish village headmanship, Scott follows through on Frey's statement by arguing that as villages become more integrated into the greater society, and as villagers recognize the advantages of extracting resources and services from various government agencies, they will begin to elect new leadership. In the place of traditional authoritarian elders, they will seek younger,[4] more sophisticated men who can interact effectively with government officials and gain needed assistance for their communities (Scott 1968).

These hypotheses are not mutually exclusive. Given different sets of circumstances, they can hold jointly or separately for various villages. In the following section, which discusses government and politics in Hayriye, we will see that both hypotheses hold, but for different periods of time.

Government and Politics in Hayriye

Prior to the establishment of the Turkish Republic and the enactment of the Village Law, the *imam* (Muslim prayer leader) in Hayriye had broad responsibilities.[5] He performed the standard religious duties, such as singing out the *ezan* ("call to prayer"), leading the *namaz* ("prayer") in the mosque, ritually washing and burying the dead, teaching the *Quran*, and so forth. He also performed ethnoreligious functions, such as writing *muskas* ("amulets") and recommending folk remedies for the village ill. Additionally, the *imam* carried out civil duties: he prepared birth and death certificates, notorized documents with an official seal, performed marriage ceremonies which had both religious and civil validity, and taught village boys reading, writing, and some other secular subjects in his mosque school.

The villagers hired the *imam* and paid his salary themselves on an annual basis. Each year, the village's household heads gathered together outside the mosque or by the *şadirvan* ("fountain for ritual ablutions") to discuss the imamship. If they were satisfied with their current *imam*, and if he wanted to stay in the village, they routinely rehired him for another year at the customary rate of about 80 *kile* of wheat a year. (A *kile* is about 30 kilos locally.) If the villagers were dissatisfied with their *imam*, or if he were leaving the post of his own will, they would already have had word sent to the *müfti* ("chief religious office holder of the province") and to area villages that Hayriye was seeking another *imam*. On the occasion of this gathering, they discussed the merits of the candidates who had applied for the post. The influential household heads did most of the talking, each stating his position in a manner both decisive and flexible, so as to facilitate an eventual consensus. As they spoke, others made consenting murmurs and finally, without the necessity of a vote, the group agreed on one of the candidates.

During these years Hayriye villagers selected their headmen in about the same manner. They, or more precisely, the important household heads, selected men who were wealthy, esteemed, and influential enough to deal effectively with visiting government officials, whom the headmen had to meet, entertain, assist, and occasionally impede. Poor and uninfluential men were never selected for this prestigeous position, which lacked much official authority.

However, the Village Law and the various secular reforms legislated during the early years of the Turkish Republic changed the relative nature of these two village posts by strictly limiting the *imam*'s responsibilities while simultaneously expanding those of the headman. For example, the *imam*'s religious lessons and folk medical practice were prohibited, his marriage ritual lost its legal recognition, and his authority to notorize and seal certificates and documents was transferred to the village headman.

With the exception of the legally instituted secret ballot, headman selection in Hayriye continued in the customary manner with the usual results. Hayriye men also elected two household heads from each of the village's five quarters to serve on the Council of Elders. The five with the most votes served as regular Council members; the second five acted as reserves or substitutes. Although the headman receives 100 *kile* of wheat annually from the villagers in addition to small fees for his notarization services, Council members serve without compensation. *Ex officio* members, the teacher and *imam,* receive salaries from the state government. (Until about 1966, however, the villagers still paid the *imam* his customary 80 *kile* of wheat each year.) The councilmen's main duties were and continue to be advising the headman, deciding on communal work projects (e.g., repairing the village's school and roads), settling local disputes, and assessing a village tax (*salma*) on each household. Because of inflation the TL20 maximum of the *salma* (fixed by a 1939 amendment) had proven grossly insufficient for village needs and this required the Council frequently to impose additional assessments for special village projects. (Only in recent years has the *salma*'s maximum been officially increased to TL200.) Those villagers who object to the amount of their tax assessment can first appeal to the Council, and then if still dissatisfied to the *kaymakam* ("subprovincial governor").

Additionally, the Council of Elders must, by law, engage a village watchman (*bekçi*) who works under the command of the headman (Section 72) to "protect the honor, life and property of everyone within the village boundary" (Section 68). In certain respects, the personal qualities of a watchman contrast with those of the headman. Rather than being wealthy and dominant, the watchman is usually poor and subordinate. The watchman's tedious and unpleasant duties make his annual salary of 70 *kile* of wheat attractive only to the village's humblest men. The watchman is selected by the village Council, certified by the *kaymakam*, paid by the village, and armed by the state. His ordinary duties include: touring the village gardens and fields during the day and night; taking into custody any persons caught stealing; impounding any animals found illegally trespassing and damaging crops; collecting fines and damages imposed by the headman on owners of trespassing animals; notifying the headman of the arrival of any official visitors to the village; spreading news and information from quarter to quarter at the headman's command; and fetching persons in the village that the headman wants to speak with.

In many respects, the administrative-political order of the village reaffirms local statuses and rankings in a way similarly achieved by the Miracle Play of Husain as celebrated in the Shi'ite village studied by Emrys Peters (1963). The village's chief figures, the heads of the dominant families, traditionally have been strongly represented in the headmanship and Council of Elders. Because they controlled the main economic resources of the village (primarily in terms of land and animals), social stability was to their advantage. They not only occupied the highest statuses of the village, but represented the village's main link with the country ruling elite, the state bureaucrats and RPP members. Until 1950, an alliance or understanding existed between the two, such that the village leaders cooperated with the government and received the full backing of the gendarmes to help maintain the social order.

The *ex officio* members of the Council represent two different historical directions, one past, the other future. The *imam*'s presence reaffirms the traditional place of Islam in the order of village life, while the secular teacher has been placed on the Council by the state government to instill modernization into its deliberations. The Turkish reformers regarded their specially trained village teachers as the prime agents of rural change. They were to transform the "backward" peasant mentality into a modern, progressive mode. However, because they are educated outsiders assigned to villages by the Ministry of Education without local consultation, villagers view them with caution, even suspicion, and the teachers' role on the Council is often ineffectual. (For a fascinating first person account of a reform-minded teacher's experiences in a very poor, traditional village, see Makal [1954]).

The holders of all village offices (with the exception of the teacher on the Council) are determined by male household heads. Women, who hold a subordinate position in society, neither attend nor indirectly participate in the meetings of the village association. Young men, who must be deferential to their elders, may attend such meetings, but usually do not speak. Poor household heads attend and may speak, however, they prefer to limit their remarks to agreements with positions already expressed by dominant household heads. Hence, the actual village association and the administration which it sanctions perpetuate the customary rank order of socioeconomic relationships.

Significantly, when any danger occurs to the property which supports the village's socioeconomic rankings, it is the watchman, a symbolic representative of the village poor, who must act as if to reestablish the sacred order. Although he may have little or no property of his own, he is officially armed and sanctioned to use force, if necessary, to protect the economic order which has relegated him to a low position. Should actual damage to someone's property occur, the headman imposes punitive fines and restitutive damages, but again it is the poor watchman who must collect them, and by so doing impress upon his fellow villagers the consequences of disturbing the sociomaterial order of things.

This system continued much as described until 1950, the year multiparty politics received its first real trial in Turkey. Political dissidents around the country and especially in the villages rallied behind the Democrats. In Hayriye social differences took on political expression as the majority of middle- and low-income villagers opposed the traditional ruling elite and protested against the existing sociopolitical system by electing their own headman on the Democrat's ticket.

Significantly, the Democratic headman belonged to a prominent lineage, from which four Republican headmen had previously come. In Hayriye kin ties cross socioeconomic and political boundries, thereby preventing the development of deep political cleavages. Owing to active campaigning by the energetic Democrats and stunned inaction on the part of the Republicans (who were unaccustomed to soliciting votes) the Democratic headman was maintained in office throughout the 1950s.

However, after overthrowing the Democrats in 1960, the ruling military junta replaced most DP headmen with persons more acceptable to their views, and the Hayriye headman was forced to give way to his patrilateral cousin—a Republican. Although the Republicans held on to the headmanship for the next three elections, there were two important differences in their style of government. First, they had learned the necessity of soliciting votes, however humbling the task might be. And second, they chose headmen of superior leadership ability, who were also much more open and democratic than their authoritarian predecessors.

The opposition did not regain the headmanship until 1973 when they elected a man who identified with the Justice Party (the DP's successor) and belonged to a lineage that had never had a headman. Party politics remained lively in village elections for about a decade after the 1960 coup despite the legal prohibition on party organization at the village level.

It appears that throughout the pre-1950 period elected officials in Hayriye represented the elitist element of the existing socioeconomic order, and consequently this period conforms closely to Kiray's status quo hypothesis. During the 1950s, however, multiparty politics permitted some change by allowing common people a greater voice in local and national government. Despite this, the village's basic system of socio-economic relations remained intact. Real change was not initiated until 1965 during the headmanship of a traditional village *ağa*, who identified with the RPP. This headman enthusiastically supported Ahmet Ozkan and his efforts to organize a cooperative by which villagers could temporarily emigrate to Europe for work. Rather than function to maintain the status quo, this well-intentioned *ağa* devoted his organizational and leadership talents to changing extensively the traditional order. As a consequence of European emigration (to be discussed more fully in a later chapter) traditional socioeconomic rankings in Hayriye have been almost completely obliterated. Many families that were formerly poor and had to labor for others, now work little or not at all. Instead of plowing soil and hoeing fields, they bask in the sun, having been made financially secure by a steady flow of marks from kin working in Germany. Ironically, one day in 1974 while a Hayriye villager and I were talking together on a village path, we observed the 1965 headman walking wearily home from his fields. "Look at him," the villager chuckled, "he used to be the village lord. Now all his land means nothing. There's no one left to work it for him."

The present headman, who was elected in 1973, appears to correspond well with the development model of headmen proposed by Scott. He is comparatively young (in his early forties) and believes that his Justice Party affiliation can be employed to the village's advantage. To achieve this advantage, he travels frequently to Inegöl to meet with government officials and fellow party members.

Most recently, partisan politics in Hayriye seems to have lost its intensity. Because the source of most families' economic security lies outside the village in Germany, many villagers (probably most) have become externally oriented and unwilling to devote much time and energy to village administration.

NOTES

1. This and subsequent references to the village law come from the English translation offered in Robinson (1949).

2. According to a Village Law revision, headmen must be literate. Although this requirement is often officially ignored, cases are known in

Table 11
Hayriye Headmen

First Name	Georgian Lineage Name	Party Affiliation[1]	Initial Year of Office
Cemil	Ortalişvili	Justice	1973
Yusuf	Malakmadze	Republican	1969
Sami	Hinkiladze	Republican	1967
Sabri	Pepunidze	Republican	1964
Sabri	Hinkiladze	Republican	1960
Omer	Hinkiladze	Democrat	1950
Şükrü	Hinkiladze	Republican	1946
Zülker	Basiladze		1940
Süleyman	Kirkitadze		1936
Kara Huseyin	Hinkiladze		1934
Mehmet	Kirnateli		1930
Huseyin	Gurgenidze		1928
Resul[2]			1925
Molla Huseyin	(not known)		1921
Haci Huseyin	Pepunidze		1919
Mercan Usta	Gurgenadze		1918
Hasan	Hinkiladze		1916

[1]From 1960 to 1973 headmen were legally prohibited from running for office on political party slates. However, because their party affiliations were known and important in village elections, they are included here.

Although candidates for headman did not run as members of a political party prior to 1946, most, if not all, were supporters of the Republican People's Party, the country's only party.

[2]Resul was a Laz, and therefore did not have a Georgian lineage name.

Source: Ahmet Ozkan's field notes and examination of village records.

which elections have been nullified by higher government officials because the victorious candidates were illiterate (Scott 1968:15).

3. In 1928 Turkey officially abandoned the use of the Arabic script for a much more efficient Latin alphabet.

4. Currently, the minimum age requirement of a headman is 25 years. Of the 216 headmen included in the 1968 village survey 69.9% were between 30 and 49 years old; 8.8% were under 30; and only 3.7% were 60 or older (*Modernization* 1974:197).

5. The following description of early village administration is based largely on the oral history supplied by elderly village residents.

7

Education,
Ethnic Identity,
and Assimilation

Education

Originally, the prime purpose of formal education in Hayriye was to turn children into good Muslims. The villagers built a small mosque in 1895 and hired a Georgian *hoja* ("religious teacher")[1] to provide religious instruction for their children and to teach their boys to read and write Ottoman Turkish as well. During the early part of the twentieth century, several village boys continued their educations in the *medrese*s (theological schools) of Istanbul. One of them eventually became a judge, first in the Ottoman, and then in the Republican judiciary, The Hayriye boys studying in Istanbul roomed with other Georgian students from different parts of Turkey. For about two centuries Georgian boys from Batumi and its hinterland had been going to Istanbul for theological studies. They had established a tradition which was continued even after the Russion capture of Batumi and the Georgian emigration to Turkey.

With the creation of the Turkish Republic following the Ottoman Empire's defeat and partition in World War I, the character and purpose of

109

Fig. 28   *Imam* in Hayriye Mosque

education in Turkey changed radically. Mustafa Kemal Ataturk, the creator and head of new Turkey, attributed the Empire's decay to Islamic-Ottoman institutions and Muslim culture. He embarked on a revolutionary program to transform "Oriental" minds and the traditional, Islamic basis of society. Members of his Republican People's Party designed a nationwide system of compulsory, secular education to socialize a new generation in accordance with the principles of modern Turkish nationalism. "Since the emergence of the idea of a Turkish national state, Turkish leaders have conceived of the schools as prime agencies in developing national consciousness, ideologies, values, and behaviors different from what had existed before and aimed at the over-all transformation of the political ethic of the country" (Kazamias 1966:220).

Following governmental actions disestablishing Islam as the state religion and substituting the Latin alphabet for the Arabic script, Hayriye's religious school was officially closed, and the hoja began teaching the new writing system along with a more general, secular curriculum. Despite government restrictions, however, the villagers refused to deny their children a religious education; they had Islamic instruction continued in secret.

In 1937 the villagers constructed a primary school (*ilk okul*, grades 1-5) on a hill in Central Quarter. They claim to have built it solely with communal labor (*imece*) and without outside government assistance. At first, the nonindigenous teachers assigned to the school by the Ministry of Education in Ankara taught only boys from Hayriye and the nearby villages lacking schools of their own. Eventually parents began sending their daughters also. Progressive parents acted on their own volition, while conservative ones reluctantly responded to the government's enforcement of the compulsory attendance law. The curriculum included Turkish language, history, geography, natural sciences, writing, arithmetic, and agriculture. Then as now, a large proportion of instructional time was devoted to Turkish language, because most Hayriye children begin school knowing only Georgian.

By the 1960s all district villages had primary schools of their own, so outside students ceased coming to Hayriye. In 1974 the Hayriye school had about 100 students and four teachers, none of whom were indigenous or Georgian. All of the village's boys and all but three or four of its girls were in attendance.

The school has had a great impact on the fates of many village males. One 67 year old Georgian man described how the school influenced the lives of his brothers:

Formerly there were many valuable and esteemed teachers here. My father had died and I, being the oldest son, did most of the farm work. We were waiting for my younger brother to finish primary school so he could help me full-time. My mother would say to him, 'Finish school and help your poor *ağabey* [big brother].' However, when he finally graduated, he was first in his class, and he refused to stay home. He left and attended middle school [*orta okul*] in Inegöl with the help of his teacher's money. We cursed him. My mother said, '*Sütüm haram olsun!*' [This is an extremely bad curse in Turkish meaning something like, 'May God punish you for suckling my milk!'] But he went on anyway. After Inegöl, he went to military school. Now he's a general. The same happened with my youngest brother. He refused to stay in the village; now he's a doctor. And here I am, still working my father's land.

By contrast, formal instruction in Hayriye has helped women only indirectly. A female informant in her thirties explained her experience with village education and her ambitions for her children to me as follows:

During my childhood village girls generally were not sent to school. I went a few times, but my father told me there was no need. "You're a girl," he said. Parents were afraid girls would learn to write and then would correspond with boys. Or at least, that's what they said. I tried learning to read on my own, but failed. Later girls went to primary school, but they didn't continue thereafter. The nearest middle school is in Inegöl, and parents will not send their daughters that far. We didn't send my oldest daughter for that reason. Because of my brother-in-law's encouragement, however, we decided to send my second daughter to live with his family in Bursa so she could attend middle school. I wanted her to have what I couldn't—an education. I wanted her to become a fine, upstanding person. Unfortunately, she was so poorly prepared, she couldn't do the work. We hope to educate our son.

In the past, many educated people came out of this village. Then the youth got lazy. Now they are beginning to wake up. Those who have succeeded try to save some of our village children.

Many older villagers say that the village teachers of the past were excellent: they inspired students and thoroughly prepared them for advanced education. Villagers praise the hoja, who taught their children in the 1920s and 1930s. Long since retired, this hoja was in his eighties and still living in Hayriye in 1974. He hardly conforms to the stereotype of the narrow-minded paragon of conservatism. He has a quick mind, a broad knowledge of the world, and, like Ataturk, he admires Western civilization. Quite frequently, he sits in one of the village coffeehouses discoursing on politics, religion, and philosophy with anyone who cares to argue or listen. One day, while discussing differences between the Muslim Middle East and the Christian West, he told me, "You killed your priests and got ahead of

Fig. 29　Quranic lesson

Fig. 30　Resting after chores

us. Now we're killing our hojas to catch up." He was referring to the European Reformation and the Turkish secularistic movement of the first half of the twentieth century. He proclaimed that the world's two greatest men are the Protestant Martin Luther and the romantic Jean Jacques Rousseau. The hoja is a devout Muslim, who believes the clergy misused Islam in the past. He opposes the idea of an Islamic hierarchy, claiming much as Rousseau did, that institutions based on inequality of status are unjust. For him religion is a matter of individual conscience; each person should relate to God directly.

Villagers also praise the earlier secular teachers, claiming they helped Hayriye produce more successful men than any other village in the district. The facts support their claim. It was not unusual for village males who graduated Hayriye's primary school in the 1930s and 1940s to leave the village in order to continue their educations. That generation of village emigrants produced at least one doctor, one army general, two army colonels, several noncommissioned officers, two engineers, several government forestry officials, several teachers, one police chief, and one *imam*. (These are conservative figures; the actual numbers achieving professional and skilled status may be higher.)

These men demonstrated a strong drive to succeed outside the village context. They developed a need to achieve that often conflicted with the expectations of their immediate kin. Their village teachers certainly share some responsibility for this. They may have been instilled with a missionary zeal, not uncommon for the time (see Makal 1954; Kirby 1960), to transform "ignorant" village youths into progressive modern men, all in accordance with Kemal Ataturk's nationalist ideology. The political scientist Lenczowski believes "the secret of Kemal's success may largely be atrributed to the strict enforcement of educational reform. The new generation of village and high school teachers constituted, with the People's Party members, a zealous cadre which spread Kemalist ideas and trained the minds of Turkish youth. Teachers became Kemal's most devoted propagandists . . . ." (as quoted in Frey 1964:223-24).

In contrast to the villagers' high evaluations of past teachers are their low assessments of more recent ones. Villagers complain that the quality of education has declined since the early 1950s. Interestingly, 1950 marked the defeat of Ataturk's Republican People's Party in the country's first truly open election. The victorious Democratic Party adopted a *laissez faire* policy with respect to business and religious expression. It also closed the village institutes, which had produced many of the village teachers most committed to Ataturk's secular and nationalistic ideology.

Villagers also say that proportionally fewer children have been going on to advanced education. Some parents blame the teachers for this, others say the children lack the necessary drive. In the period between 1972-74, no graduates of the village school had successfully continued on to middle school. Several had tried, but failed.

Those who were fortunate enough to get an education and escape village life during the early decades have remained in the cities, and most have done little or nothing to change conditions back in the village. With the exception of labor emigration to Europe in the 1960s, village life has continued much as before, with each new generation beginning from the same starting block. Some successful emigrants have tried "to save" nieces and nephews in Hayriye by convincing their parents to let the children join them in the city where they can attend school. In this way, a few dozen village children have joined the ranks of the educated.

Of the village's adult population in 1974, an estimated 65% to 70% of the men and 45% to 50% of the women were functionally literate in Turkish. During the same year, about a dozen children, mostly girls, were enrolled in the village *imam's* Quranic course (see Figure 29).

Ethnic Identity and Assimilation

Although details of the flight of Georgian, Circassian, and other Caucasian people to Turkey in the second half of the nineteenth century comprise some of the most dramatic pages of late Ottoman history, precious little is known about the subsequent assimilation of these people. Even their numbers can only be guessed at because Turkey's official censuses do not list people by their ethnic background but rather by the languages which they purportedly claim as their mother tongues. Commenting on the reliability of similar census data, Sabahattin Alpat (President of the Turkish State Institute of Statistics) has written that "pre-tests carried out before the censuses showed that the information given about residence and the period of residence, number of marriages, births, and marriage age were answered either incorrectly or incompletely" (1969:61). He further complained of the difficulty in finding qualified personnel to conduct the census, especially in the villages where the bulk of the population lives. When we add to these considerations the general tendency on the part of non-Turks to claim Turkish as their mother tongue for social reasons, we must conclude that official statistics by mother tongue are poor indicators of the actual number of the various non-Turkish peoples in Turkey.

Table 12 contains official statistics for various census years of the number of people in Turkey claiming Georgian either as their mother tongue or as their second language. Very probably, most of these latter people are Georgian also. Intercensus fluctuations partly, or largely, derive from the uneven quality of the different censuses.

Table 12
People in Turkey Claiming Georgian as Their Mother
Tongue or Second Language

	1935	1945	1955	1960	1965
Mother Tongue	57,325	40,076	52,000	33,000	34,330
Second Language	16,000	9,000	47,000	29,000	48,976

Sources: *1959, Türkiye Istatistik Yıllığı* (Ankara, 1959), p. 81.

1960, Türkiye Cumhuriyeti Istatistik Yıllığı (Ankara, 1962), p. 79.

1965, Genel Nüfus Sayımı (Ankara, 1969), pp. 178-179.

De Vos defines ethnic identity as a people's subjective symbolic or emblematic use of any aspect of their culture in order to differentiate themselves from others (1975:16). He also writes that "an ethnic group is a self-perceived group of people who hold in common a set of traditions not shared by others with whom they are in contact" (ibid. 9). Utilizing these definitions, I would consider the Georgians of Hayriye a people with a partial ethnic identity. Although they regard themselves as Georgians, they also identify as Muslims and Turkish citizens. These second and third identities constitute strong assimilative forces. In fact, the degree to which Hayriye Georgians have been absorbed into Turkish culture and society is quite high.

Being pious Muslims, they share with the Turks the same moral code or constellation of sociocultural values embodied in their common religion. The two peoples are members of a Muslim brotherhood and accept the same Islamic criteria for the evaluation of life. These commonalities facilitate mutual understanding and interethnic cohesion. Any Turk visiting the village is welcomed in the mosque. Likewise, any Georgian traveling or relocating outside Hayriye is readily accepted as a prayer companion by the Turks.

Georgian assimilation throughout Turkey has also been influenced by the official position of the Turkish government, especially during the early years of the Republic when the establishment of a Turkish national homeland and spirit was of critical importance. According to official histories, all Muslim people living in Turkey are racially and ethnically Turks. Georgian and Circassian are said to be mere dialects of Turkish, and their use in public places is not condoned. This official ideology is inculcated in the public schools and appears to be generally accepted by many Georgians in Turkey. For instance, in the not-too-distant town of Susurluk, one primary school teacher of Georgian extraction told me that Georgians are really Caspian Turks who speak a Turkish dialect which they should now replace with standard Turkish. As an educational leader in his community, his opinion carries great weight.

All Hayriye Georgians regularly speak Georgian with kin and fellow villagers, but none could read it even if publications were available. Many can, however, read Turkish. In addition to being the "school" language, Turkish is also the "work" language. Anyone employed in the village by the Turkish Forestry Service or outside the village by almost any firm must understand and speak Turkish. Many of the offspring of those who have emigrated to cities over the years have grown up knowing only Turkish. When they visit Hayriye to see relatives, they cannot participate in the villagers' customary mode of communication. As a result, almost all intercourse with people residing outside Hayriye, even though they are kin, is via Turkish. For these reasons, Georgian functions as a symbol of identity primarily in Hayriye's familial and informal settings. By necessity, practically all Georgian villagers learn Turkish at an early age, and by the time they are young adults most speak it as well as Turks of similar educational background. A Georgian can, however, frequently be distinguished from a Turk by the throaty quality of his speech and his tendency to pronounce the initial /f/ sound as /p/.

Turkey's compulsory military service also functions to channel Georgians and other minorities into a more unified stream of Turkish society and culture. During his early twenties, practically every Hayriye male leaves the village and joins the Turkish Army for a two year experience in patriotism. The following observation, made by Paul Stirling (1965:270) as he studied a Turkish village in the early 1950s, holds as well for Hayriye:

> Undoubtedly military service was a major cause of the village's unquestioned identification with the national state, and a source, through indoctrination, of glory in Turkey's achievements. Almost all had an opportunity to see more of Turkey, and a few learned literacy and technical skills.

Here we must add that the process of Georgian assimilation has been facilitated by the openness and general tolerance of the Turks, who have welcomed these Muslim immigrants into their homeland and accepted them. Georgians have not been barred from political or social organizations or occupational groups. Many who have left Hayriye now hold prominent positions in Turkish society.

For the perpetuation of an ethnic identity, distinctive physical characteristics and endogamy, or strong identification with an ancestral homeland, or special cultural traditions such as unique rites of passage, dress, and food, may separately or jointly be more important than language. With respect to Hayriye Georgians, none of these elements has the full force of separation, and some have contributed to assimilation.

Although Hayriye villagers have traditionally favored intraethnic marriages, marital unions with non-Georgians have occurred and their rate is increasing, thereby speeding the process of integration. Physically, Georgians are not very different from many Turks, although they tend to be more European in appearance. Generally, they have light to medium complexions and medium to tall statures (5'6" to 5'10" for men). Brown, blue, and green eyes, brunette and blond hair are common among them. Many of the men have deeply set eyes, protruding chins, and hooked noses (see Figure 30). On the whole, Turks regard Georgians as an attractive people, which partly explains their willingness, even desire, to marry them.

With reference to rites of passage, food, and dress, Hayriye villagers resemble Turks in most respects. Although they maintain certain elements of cultural uniqueness, these do not function to sharply separate them from others. Over the generations they have tended to blend their Georgian ways with Turkish ones. Hayriye Georgians do recognize an ancestral territory, but this recognition serves both to integrate them with the Turks as well as to separate them. When they refer to their original homeland (which now lies in the Turkish province of Artvin) as "the most civilized part of Turkey," they evince no feeling of national separateness. On the contrary, they appear to express a conceptual congruence between the land of their ancestors and the land of their citizenship. In the first instance they exhibit pride; in the second they admit to reality.

NOTE

1. In Hayriye, as in many villages in Turkey, the titles *hoja* and *imam* are used interchangeably.

8

Village Organizational Efforts and Large-Scale Emigration

Up until the 1950s socioeconomic relations in Hayriye were structured primarily by agnation, affinity, and common village residence. Kin and neighbors cooperated informally to solve the economic exigencies of existence and to perform the ritual requisites of passage through the life-cycle. As the twentieth century moved into its second half, various attempts were made to add formal structures to the organization of village life. In the following pages Ahemt Ozkan describes these efforts and offers his personal assessment of the obstacles, failures, and successes involved. Ozkan's interpretation of events is especially revealing because he himself was one of their prime movers. I have translated his commentary from Turkish into English, placing my own additions in brackets.

> Since the very beginning of Hayriye the villagers have placed great emphasis on education. During the time of the sultans, village boys were sent to the theology schools of Istanbul. The villagers even increased their stress on education in the republican period. Over the years many educated people have emerged from Hayriye: a doctor, a general, several colonels, engineers, teachers, accountants, etc. But all

119

of these people leave the village; some never return, others come back only to visit on special holidays and for weddings and funerals. All of them must remember the village water they drank, the air they breathed, the bread they ate, the pleasant and painful experiences of their youth. Yet, they rarely think of doing something for the village. How many times have I heard them complain:"It's easy to get from any corner of Turkey to Inegöl, but getting from Inegöl to Hayriye is a problem!" Still they don't think about helping to solve the village's road problem or its need for better drinking water and modern agricultural methods.

Only Faik Ertan, a young man from the village who had become a teacher in Istanbul, decided to organize a development association to deal with village needs. He sent letters to all of Hayriye's educated emigrants, asking them to meet in the village to discuss its problems and possible solutions with local residents. A number took up his suggestion and the meeting was held in 1954. For the first time ever, emigrants and residents got together to talk over village issues.

They discussed the creation of a development association and its objectives. Some argued for dealing with all of the village's economic and educational problems on a broad front. Others wanted to confine themselves to a narrow range of problems. Some said that the government should carry out the necessary development programs. Others warned against too much government involvement, but were themselves unwilling to invest all the time and money necessary. Some villagers felt uneasy about Ertan, because he had been away from the village so long. They accused him of organizing the meeting for ulterior motives, such as promoting an imagined future candidacy for parliament. In addition, a few of the emigrants may have begrudged Ertan for taking an initiative they had not. In this atmosphere of disagreement and suspicion, organizing an association was impossible.

Not being from Hayriye, I knew nothing of this meeting. In 1955 I married a woman originally from the village, and during our visits to her family in Hayriye I developed an attachment to the people and their way of life. Consequently, our visits became more frequent. In the summer of 1960, I was doing an apprenticeship in Bursa's Public Works Office as an architectural student from Istanbul Technical University. In accordance with a decision of the Provincial Council, I and other apprentices were assigned the duty of going to different villages in the province to explain the goals of the revolutionary government [There had been a military coup in 1960.], listen to the villagers' needs and petitions, and prepare individual village reports. I immediately set off for Hayriye and arranged a general village meeting in Zeki's coffeehouse on the evening of September 9. The village men poured out their troubles. They wanted a better road to Inegöl, improved drinking water, electricity, extension courses in sewing, rug-making, building crafts, etc. I prepared a report, which was passed on to the Provincial Government through the Public Works Office. But unfortunately, the government did not react. Hayriye's problems are replicated in 40,000 Turkish villages. They have existed since the thirteenth century and have yet to be taken in hand.

But I did not let the matter drop there. I began to conduct a personal investigation of village problems with the objective of planning a sound development program. After becoming acquainted with different government agencies, I invited a group of about 15 officials from the Provincial Agricultural Office, Settlement Office, Provincial Bank, and Public Works Office to tour Hayriye and offer advice. They came, inspected the village and its surroundings, and made suggestions.

Meanwhile, Faik Ertan had learned of my activities and dropped in on me in Bursa. After introducing himself, he described his disappointing attempt to organize a village development association. Then he suggested that the two of us try again, and I agreed. This time, villagers who were impressed with my previous efforts in Hayriye supported us, and we successfully organized the Hayriye Education and Development Association in 1961.

Over the next several years the association engaged in a number of economic and cultural projects. The following are among the most noteworthy:

1. Village map preparation. Before planning a village development project, a map showing the village's settlement pattern and topography is essential. Upon the association's formal request, the Turkish Air Squadron in Eskişehir took aerial photographs of Hayriye and sent them to us. From the photographs I prepared a village map.

2. Architectural, sociocultural, and economic studies. Upon my recommendation, students from the Architectural Faculty of Istanbul Technical University took on Hayriye as a research project in 1961. They studied the village and drew up plans for certain facilities which the village lacked, such as a guest house, clinic, public bath, and meeting hall.

Also upon my suggestion, a group of graduate students and professors from the Engineering Faculty and the Department of City and Regional Planning in the Architectural Faculty of Middle East Technical University (METU) selected Hayriye as a village research project. The group made several trips to the village in 1961-62 to study its economy, culture, society, and building needs. They published their research along with economic and architectural recommendations in a 1963 mimeographed report. We refer to this report when planning other projects.

3. Land development. In accordance with the research and recommendations of the METU report, our association applied to the Office of Irrigation and Drainage for assistance in land development. This office responded positively by terracing approximately 300 *dönüm*s of village land on which grapevines and apple tree saplings have been planted. [A *dönüm* is approximately 1/4 of an acre.]

4. Organizing a folk dance group. At numerous Hayriye weddings I observed native dances and listened to folk music that the villagers had brought with them from Georgia about a century before. In order to continue these folk traditions in an organized way, the association agreed to sponsor a Hayriye folk dance group. We outfitted a dozen village men with Georgian costumes, provided them with instruments, and scheduled their practice sessions. In 1963 the group entered the Bursa Folklore Festival and received high praise for its performance. [The group later disbanded when most of its members emigrated to Germany.]

5. The village folk music project. I also taped village folk songs and sent them to America where Peter Gold, a student in Indiana University's Folklore Institute, heard them and liked them. He wrote me requesting information about Georgian music. I not only answered his questions and secured pertinent books for him, but the association and I arranged his visit to Hayriye so that he could tape village songs himself. I translated the taped songs from Georgian into French and provided him with village photographs. The final result of all this work was a beautiful record: "Georgian Folk Music from Turkey" [Distributed by Anthology Record and Tape Corp., U.S.A.].

6. A village reading room. During the early 1960s the association constructed a village reading room and supplied it with the help of Faik Ertan. The villagers put up a small, two-story building with a large reading room on the second floor. They furnished the room with shelves, tables, chairs, a wood-burning stove, and a pressurized kerosene lamp. Ertan conducted a book drive among book sellers in Istanbul, Ankara, and Bursa which brought in hundreds of volumes. The village's young men ran the reading room; they elected officers, registered books, and checked them in and out. The reading room provided Hayriye with a needed educational and cultural opportunity. [According to the METU report, the reading room was used mostly during the slack agricultural months of December, January, and February and least during the busy months of July, August, and September. Elderly men preferred books on religion and agriculture, while young men usually chose novels, and children borrowed school-related books. Although women and girls did not go to the reading room, some did send their brothers, sons, or husbands to borrow books for them. Unfortunately, the reading room building was condemned in the late 1960s because of a landslide near its edge. By 1974 a replacement facility had still not been erected.]

7. In 1964 members of the Hayriye association got together with representatives from Bahariye, Konurlar, and Murat Bey—three of the villages sharing the road to Inegöl—and petitioned the Department of Provincial and Village Roads for help with road construction. The petition was favorably received, and communal labor from the four villages was coordinated with men and equipment from the Road Department and the Forestry Office to improve that portion of the Inegöl road from Ortaköy to Muratbey [see Map B]. [Portions of this road are still washed away each year. Ultimately, the road needs an improved stone bed and pavement.]

It seems unlikely that many of the association's accomplishments could have been realized without the leadership of men like Ahmet Ozkan and Faik Ertan, who possess special organizational talents, advanced education, and bureaucratic experience. It is a credit to the less worldly-wise village leaders who supported and contributed to the efforts of these men. Significantly, Ahmet Ozkan's own father-in-law was the village chief (*muhtar*) from 1964 to 1967—an extremely critical period in the village's development. However important the association's early activities may appear, the villagers' lives did not begin to change significantly until the advent of further organizational developments in 1965.

The Hayriye Development Cooperative

In 1964 Ozkan tried to excite the villagers about the possibility of forming an agricultural cooperative so that they could pool and then sell their produce without the necessity of losing money to middlemen. Although about 26 village men initially agreed to form the cooperative, later at least half of them refused to cooperate. From this experience, the architect concluded (much as the anthropologist George Foster (1967) did about the Mexican peasants of Tzintzuntzan) that the villagers' mentality was not conducive to formalized cooperative action, that their deep-seated mutual suspicions and individualism were obstacles to cooperative village development. In addition to these impediments, the middlemen who customarily bought from the villagers contributed to the cooperative's demise by claiming it was communistic. Apparently, the cooperative conflicted with the established structure of economic relationships that had resulted from years of social maneuvering. The supportive half of the original membership consisted of men who were either related to Ahmet affinally or who had become his friends. They promised to make the cooperative work, but it remained dormant nevertheless.

In that same year the Turkish government announced that it would grant priority for purposes of worker emigration to mountain and forest villages that established development cooperatives which would: 1) submit the names of villagers desiring to emigrate, 2) collect remittances from successfully employed emigrants, and 3) use the remittances for village development projects. Reportedly, mountain and forest villages were given priority because they tend to be poorer than plain villages, and many infringe on government forests.

Due to high levels of unemployment and underemployment in Turkey and the need for inexpensive labor in the expanding economies of Europe, Turkish workers had begun emigrating to Europe in the early 1960s. Turkey had concluded her first agreement to supply workers to a foreign country with the Federal Republic of Germany in October, 1961. Since then, she has signed similar agreements with Austria, Belgium, the

Netherlands, France, Sweden, and Australia. Reports from early emigrants about European pay scales, working conditions, and their own ability to save were so positive that a craze to emigrate soon developed in Turkey. West Germany has been the dominant host country, absorbing about 90% of the approximately one million Turks who have emigrated up to 1974. In that year, another million Turks hoping to emigrate were on official waiting lists.

The Turkish political scientist, N. Abadan-Unat, describes what she regards as the major "push-pull" factors affecting Turkish emigration on a nation-wide basis (1974:386):

> Contemporary migrant workers have one dominating, conscious wish: to make as much money as possible as quickly as possible. This strong desire is propagated and cultivated intensively by the mass media, which contribute to enlarging the circle of those with "rising expectations". Stereotypes, higher standards of living, and social welfare inspire most of the migrant workers. Of course, [Turkey's] chronic unemployment, a weak industrial structure, the insufficiency of the national wage scale, individual frustrations, and a desire to learn about the world are also contributing factors.

The idea of promoting rural development through cooperatives received needed impetus in 1964 when Turkey's Ministry of Village Affairs was formed. The ministry devised a plan to utilize the earnings of migrant workers to improve village conditions. It encouraged residents of poor villages to organize village development cooperatives (VDCs) meeting the three conditions listed above, and then awarded such cooperatives emigration contingents or quotas so that their members could secure employment abroad without having to wait in a long line of registered hopefuls.

> The Village Development Cooperative approach had the eminent advantage of promoting the economic organization of aspirant migrants before they left Turkey, creating, it was believed, an investment target even before they had accumulated capital to take aim with. ...members securing employment abroad were to remain under an obligation to remit contributions to their VDC which would be invested in a project. Upon their return, migrant members would be the first to profit from employment opportunities created through their investments [Renselaar and Velzen 1976:105].

Ahmet Ozkan, the architect, and Faik Ertan, the teacher, interpreted the government's 1964 announcement as a wonderful opportunity for Hayriye. Sending workers to Europe would eliminate the poverty and near-subsistence lifestyle common in the village by generating needed capital· for both individual families and Hayriye as a whole. They immediately set about preparing a cooperative charter and filling out the necessary government forms. They also outlined the positive aspects of emigration to the village men. The men, however, did not require much convincing. They already knew about the success of previous emigrants from Turkey, and although their own emigration would be through a cooperative, once in Europe they would acquire individual jobs and individual pay checks. Hence, they saw a direct connection between their participation in the cooperative and their personal gain. Within a short period of time over 70 men, or about half of the males in the 20 to 39 age group, formally expressed their desire to emigrate.

The government approved Hayriye's application for a VDC[1] and awarded it a 110-person contingent, to include Hayriye members as well as people from nearby villages who join the cooperative. In November of 1965 a group of 71 Hayriye men and 39 men from neighboring villages went via the VDC to West Germany where most got jobs in manufacturing industries. Initially, many village women cursed Ozkan for sending their men to the distant "land of the non-believers," but these curses quickly changed to prayers when money began pouring into household purses. The government awarded Hayriye's VDC a second contingent of 50 persons in 1972. Consequently, 29 more Hayriye men (ranging in age from 22 to 33) together with 21 men from nearby villages went to West Germany to join their friends and relations in lucrative employment.

For decades a small but steady stream of Hayriye villagers had been emigrating to Turkish cities for better employment and living opportunities. Most of them had or soon acquired some education or skill to facilitate their adaptation to an urban environment. The cooperative, by contrast, represented the first opportunity for a large-scale emigration of unskilled village men to industrial centers. It not only intensified emigration, but extended it abroad.

It might be argued that this sudden rural exodus resulted from excessive population pressure: Hayriye's arable land could not support its over 1,000 inhabitants. To survive, some families had been forced to rent land in other villages. In addition, the village's inheritance system recognizes the right of each son remaining in Hayriye to an equal share of his father's estate. Without emigration, such an inheritance rule would eventually reduce individual land holdings to minuscule amounts. It could be argued further that Hayriye peasants had succumbed to the revolution of rising material aspirations, which can be satisfied only through emigration to urban-industrial centers. The inevitable comparisons between city and village life made Hayriye increasingly unattractive.

Although a certain amount of validity can be credited to these "push-pull" hypotheses of emigration, they are nevertheless inadequate because they treat peasants as dependent variables of change—as simple, tradition-bound reactors to circumstances beyond their control. Most Hayriye villagers have not merely *reacted* to internal and external pressures of change; they have *interacted* with them in an attempt to accomplish new personal, familial, and communal goals. Collectively and individually they have demonstrated an understanding of their situations, examined existing alternatives, exercised volition, and made choices. They can be regarded as *interactive* elements of change, being neither completely subject to nor in control of their situations. They have modified alternatives, created new strategies, and established new networks in order to achieve desired goals. The interactive nature of their participation in change will become more evident in the following chapters which analyze their international emigration and its consequences.

NOTE

1. Renselaar and Velzen (1976:107) report that "in 1965 alone 250 VDC's were constituted, far more than the ministry of Village Affairs could possibly assist with meaningful planning." Hayriye villagers claim theirs was the 16th such VDC formed.

9

An Analysis of Emigration

To facilitate an understanding of the complex phenomenon under consideration, an effort is made in this chapter to explain the "model of man"[1] utilized in this study. Not being a believer in the concept of observer-independent truth, especially when it is applied to the study of human behavior, I feel it is important for social scientists to determine their own underlying assumptions about human nature and reveal them to their readers. Unfortunately, most social scientists fail to do this, despite the necessity of such revelations for an understanding of their logic-in-use.

The basic components of the model of man employed in this study are presented below in sequential fashion. This linear ordering was necessitated by the constraints of our written medium. Such a presentation, however, distorts the model, for in its actual application it takes on a more holistic and synchronous character. Consequently, some readers may feel that the model is not always readily apparent in the subsequent analysis. I am fairly confident, however, that with some reflective searching, they will find it. I could be completely confident if I believed in the concept of observer-independent truth.

The model's basic components were derived from a number of different social and behavioral science paradigms which I found partially congruent, complementary, and/or mutually supporting. The resulting construct is the product of a type of general systems thinking (cf. Bertalanffy 1968), and its emphasis on self conception, purposive behavior, and teleology makes it compatible with certain extant theories: two being Talcott Parsons' general theory of action and identity-interaction theory (see Robbins 1973). The model can also be fruitfully employed in conjunction with some existing models of migration, such as those described by du Toit (1975) and Cardona and Simmons (1975).

After explaining the "model of man in change," the chapter continues with a discussion of migrant ideology and community goals.

A Model of Man in Change—An Explanatory Scheme

A model of man is comprised of "a selective set of propositions whose purpose is not to exhaustively describe or define all of the nature of man, but to make statements concerning those aspects of individuals which are necessary for subsequent theoretical and practical issues" (Kunkel 1970:17). The model may characterize aspects of human personality and also include propositions about relationships between human behavior and various sociocultural contexts. Hence, the model is a basic part of an explanatory scheme. While it may be considered the "given" of a particular analysis, its general status is that of a hypothesis whose components are subject to change as new knowledge warrants.

For the purposes of this study, I have conceptualized a "model of man in change", which draws heavily on a number of sources: humanistic psychology, humanistic anthropology, learning theory, reference group theory, and modeling theory. The resulting construct is, I believe, especially well-suited to the analysis and explanation of sociocultural change involving most twentieth century people. As I sequentially describe and interrelate the model's various components below, I name a few psychologists, sociologists, and anthropologists, who have defined or employed one or more of this model's basic parts. I do this primarily to explicate the model, and unless specifically stated, I do not assume that the persons mentioned necessarily originated the ideas involved.

The Humanistic Component. The model's personality component could have been derived from the work of almost any one of the major humanistic psychologists. However, I have chosen the goal-oriented Individual Psychology of Alfred Adler (1956), which views each person holistically as a creative, "becoming" individual who strives to accomplish various self-selected goals within his phenomenal field. Adlerian personality theory is socioteleological; it conceives of man as being pulled from in front by his ambitions, rather than being pushed from behind by heredity or environment. Adlerian man actively initiates actions to improve his status. The unitary dynamic principle is life as movement in the direction of growth and expansion, life as dynamic striving from a perceived minus position to a perceived plus position. This principle implies a high degree of internal, subjective causation. Because the individual participates in the cause, he becomes the important intervening variable.

Given the gaps in our knowledge of human nature and the uncertainties involved in its explanation, this "soft deterministic" approach has been described as "one of the most valuable working concepts available" (Murphy 1947:645). Its importance has also been attested to by the psychologist Woodworth (1934), who rejected the S-R (Stimulus-Response) formula for behavior and proposed a stimulus-person-response formula in its place. Woodworth held that the response is not only a function of the stimulus, but of the individual's perception, which in turn is influenced by his personality, his goals and motivations, and his sociocultural affiliations.

Also central to Adlerian psychology is the concept of social interest, which maintains that man has an innate aptitude for social relations; he is embedded in a larger sociocultural milieu and normally will choose goals with their anticipated social consequences implicitly or explicitly in mind. Adler maintained that human existence requires each individual to face up to a basic set of life tasks or challenges: work-cooperation, society-friendship, and love-sex-marriage. That is, human existence necessitates reliance on others, cooperative and affective relations with others, and beneficial contributions to others. More recently, two of Adler's disciples, Mosak and Dreikurs, have specified a pair of additional life tasks: the first is the ontological problem of defining God and the universe and relating to them, and the second concerns coping with oneself as subject and object (Mosak and Dreikurs 1973:42). Although these life challenges are regarded as universal, human responses to them vary across as well as within cultures.

In many respects, these ideas parallel those of the anthropologist Charles Erasmus, who writes: "In this changing world of cultural behavior I view man's motivational and cognitive attributes as the active agents of causality, and his environmental conditions (both physical and cultural) as passive.... Motivation is the stimulus to action, but cognition introduces a creative element without which action would not take symbolic and cultural form" (1961:11). Although ecological, social, and technological factors affect the probability of appearance or extinction of a particular human behavior, all cultural behavior stems from individual motivation and the employment of human cognition to achieve goals within the constraints of limiting conditions.

Erasmus posits three basic motivations: (1) the desire to survive, (2) the desire for sexual gratification, and (3) the desire for prestige, social status, or achievement (1961:13). In the study of sociocultural change, the third is the most important and may be conveniently subsumed under Adler's work-society-love triad. Drawing on the work of sociologist Richard T. LaPiere and psychologist David C. McClelland, Erasmus reasons that: "Because of the long maturation period of social dependency during which the human child is subject to many tests of achievement, persons in all human societies become victims to some degree of invidious comparison and the concern for status." Hence, prestige motivation is pan-social, and "I shall view [it] as the stimulus to cultural development" (1961:13).

The individual in Erasmus' model of man is a rational being whose future actions are largely a function of his *frequency interpretations*—that is, his probability estimates (based on past observations and direct or vicarious experience) that such action will be rewarded and not punished. He will alter his behavior when his new frequency interpretations make clear connections between the alternative and a more desirable consequence. At the most general level, the individual's motive is the attainment of greater prestige or, in Adlerian terms, movement toward a perceived plus position.

The Behavioral Component. Various behavioral models of man based on learning theories and developed in experimental psychology during the past half century have become quite popular in the behavioral sciences.[2] These models postulate that most human behavior patterns are established and maintained by means of differential reinforcement. Members of a group or society generally reward only those behaviors they regard as "desirable," and punish those they deem "wrong". This differential reinforcement system usually increases the probability that individuals will repeat preferable behaviors under similar circumstances and reduces the frequency of those behaviors associated with punishment.

According to this model much of cultural behavior is established and maintained or weakened by its reinforcing or aversive consequences, called *contingent stimuli*. Among the major types of contingencies are: primary stimuli, secondary stimuli, and generalized reinforcers. Primary stimuli are largely physiologically based and include such things as food, water, and physical abuse, which maintain a general similarity from one culture to another. By contrast, secondary stimuli (e.g., verbal compliments, material goods, love) are learned, and their perceived values vary among different cultures. Of greatest importance to the study of sociocultural change are the generalized reinforcers, such as prestige and money, which can be exchanged for a wide variety of primary and secondary reinforcers.

The effectiveness of a particular reinforcing stimulus for the shaping of a new behavior depends in large part on the state variables— the individual's characteristics of deprivation and satiation with respect to the stimulus. For instance, hunger (state variable) makes immediately consumable food an effective contingency for promoting a new behavior, while satiation reduces or eliminates its effectiveness. The establishment and continuation of many or most patterns of cultural behavior depend on the maintenance of some degree of deprivation. Hence, the importance of generalized reinforcers like money and prestige. In an egalitarian society possessing a simple hunting and gathering technology and lacking a monetized system of exchange the range of reinforcers is quite limited. Consequently, it might be more difficult to shape new behavior patterns there than in a highly differentiated, monetized society, in which the maintenance of deprivation is facilitated by popular ambitions to achieve higher status and acquire more money—a generalized reinforcer whose satiation threshold is extremely high because it can buy so many other desirable items.

The behavior component of this model of man neither eliminates nor negates considerations of intercultural variablity or individual personality differences. An individual's motivations and learning history, including the internalized values and norms of his culture, all play a role in the determination of his state variables and his appraisal of any contingency. Additional considerations of importance include: environmental constraints; the individual's ability to predict, evaluate, and combine all of the relevant consequences of his actions; and the individual's capacity to perform the behavior necessary to achieve his desired goal.

Even though the learning principles or procedures utilized to construct this behavioral component appear to operate in all societies, they do not deny the existence of an individual's internal, subjective state. They do, however, help the social scientist circumvent many of the problems created by his lack of knowledge or evidence about this internal state, its operation, and its effects on behavior. The behavioral component aids immensely in the explanation of general behavioral regularities, although it is inadequate for dealing with such considerations as individual genius, spontaneity, and creativity.

The Reference Group and Modeling Components. A basic social scientific fact is that many of an individual's values, norms, attitudes, and characteristic modes of behavior are shaped by his enculturational experience and primary group memberships. It is also a fact, however, that many people (especially those in societies undergoing change) orient themselves to values, norms, attitudes, and behavior patterns other than "their own" and aspire to statuses and identities which are not part of their membership groups. This second fact constitutes the concern of *reference group theory*.

change) orient themselves to values, norms, attitudes, and behavior patterns other than "their own" and aspire to statuses and identities which are not part of their membership groups. This second fact constitutes the concern of *reference group theory*.

Reference groups have been defined as "those groups to which the individual relates himself as a member or aspires to relate himself psychologically" (Sherif and Sherif 1969:418).[3] The term *reference person* is used when the source of an individual's attitudes and goals is another person, and *reference set* is appropriately used when an individual orients himself to a category of people who do not strictly constitute a group, such as a social class, urbanites, or modern Europeans. Schmitt (1972) has subsumed these three terms under the single rubric of *reference other*, and refers to the process of identifying with or comparing oneself to others as the *reference other orientation*.

Herbert Hyman introduced the reference group concept in 1942, and during the ensuing two decades social psychologists and sociologists applied it widely. In the sixties, however, critics charged that the users of the concept had assigned it so many different referents that the term no longer had much meaning (Linn 1966). More recently, Schmitt (1972) has critically reviewed the reference group literature, including the arguments for and against its merits, and concludes that the concept is valuable if employed carefully.

I hope to avoid many of the problems associated with the concept by narrowly limiting its referents and explicitly stating its operational position in the model. Here I will limit the discussion of "reference other" conceptualization and application to several topics of central importance to this study: (1) the problem of multiple "reference others," sociocultural change, and prediction, (2) the comparative function of "reference others" and relative deprivation, and (3) the normative function of "reference others," anticipatory socialization, and modeling.

Multiple "reference others," sociocultural change, and prediction. In a closed, egalitarian society with a simple technology, people generally identify with others who are very similar to themselves. In these cases, the "reference other" concept is of limited use. However, in an open, modernizing society with a multiplicity of statuses and opportunities for social mobility, an individual may have multiple "reference others" of differential importance (ego-involvement) to him. The norms of some of these different references may be mutually incompatible, and consequently they cause the individual either to be alienated from certain groups (usually his more primary and traditional ones) or to compartmentalize his attitudes and behaviors into appropriate sociocultural contexts. An example of the second case would be a person from a peasant background who aspires to become an urbanite. In order to avoid negative sanctions, he acts like a peasant in his natal village, and like an urbanite in the city.

In this more differentiated situation the "reference other" concept not only adds to the analysis in a *ex post facto* way but also enhances predictability. By knowing the relative importance of a person's "reference others" with respect to his hierarchy of values and motivations, we improve our ability to predict the kinds of behaviors he is likely to engage in under various conditions.

The comparative functions of "reference others" and relative deprivation. Most, if not all, modernizing societies are characterized by a generalized positive value for upward mobility. Members of such societies, who have strongly internalized this value, are driven by an ambition to "improve" their socioeconomic positions and gain greater increments of prestige. When assessing their current positions these people will normally take as their standard of comparison some reference person, group, or set that stands higher than they in the social hierarchy. Consequently, they experience *relative deprivation* (Merton 1957: Ch 8). Although their past gains may have been substantial and their current positions comfortable, their motivation to rise yet higher causes them to seek out "superior" references and feel deprived by comparison.

The study by Form and Geschwender (1962) of social reference and job satisfaction among 545 manual workers in Lansing, Michigan illustrates this situation. The researchers found that those workers who generally did not anticipate further social mobility and tended to use primary group members as their comparative references were most satisfied with their job positions. By contrast, those workers who did anticipate social mobility used white collar workers, who ranked above them, as their comparative reference set and were less satisfied with their job positions. The authors conclude that, "When a working class male becomes imbued with this ideology of opportunity and upward mobility he tends to shift his social references to the incumbents of positions above him and tends to exhibit relatively more job dissatisfaction" (Form & Geschwender 1962:237).

The normative function of "reference others," anticipatory socialization, and modeling. Psychologically, the "reference other" concept is based on a person's capacity to relate himself to persons, groups, and social categories that may be absent from his environment and even remote in terms of geography and time. In his own imagination, a person can relate himself to persons he has never met and who, in turn, do not even know of his existence (Sherif & Sherif 1969:422-23). As a consequence, this person (say a peasant girl in a small, isolated village, who chooses as her reference set modern, urban women about whom she formed impressions exclusively from the cinema and magazines) may begin to shape behaviors, attitudes, and goals that she deems characteristic of her reference set, but which may conflict with local ways. This process of attitudinal and behavior change Merton (1957) terms *anticipatory socialization* and Bandura (1969) calls *modeling*. According to Merton, the individual behaves as if she is preparing herself for entrance into her reference set and hopes that by emulating the perceived characteristics of that set others will identify her as a member. The transforming peasant in our example may begin to draw such opposing contrasts between the norms or standards of her own membership group and those of her reference set, that for her the first becomes a negative reference group and the second a positive reference set. The difference being motivated rejection of her own group's norms in favor of motivated assimilation of the other's (Merton 1957:300).

Highly corroborative of reference group theory and its associated concept, anticipatory socialization, is the modeling theory of learning and behavior change described by Bandura and Walters (1963) and Bandura (1969). They point out that in all cultures motivated individuals learn vicariously by observing the behavior patterns of real-life or symbolized models. People learn in this vicarious manner in all cultures and are reinforced vicariously when they see that their models or "reference others" are rewarded for their characteristic behavioral modes. Hence, modeling and reference group theory can be used conjointly to indicate the sources of an individual's or a group's behavior standards and the agency of their reinforcement. Together with the other components of the model, these two theories can add significantly to an understanding of sociocultural change, as the following general example by Bandura (1969:199-203) illustrates:

Even the most successful sociocultural and/or economic innovations frequently involve some initial negative consequences which deter many potential adopters. The beneficial results of these innovations may not be clearly demonstrable unless they have been applied with sufficient commitment over an extended time period. Until then, people are normally reluctant to abandon existing behaviors of proven utility and expend their time, energy, and resources in newer ways with possibly superior but uncertain consequences. Their reluctance is also attributable to the fact that traditional behavior patterns are commonly fortified by belief systems and moral codes that portend hazardous consequences (physical, spiritual, and social) for those who deviate. Consequently, local innovators are often initially subjected to the negative sanctions of their neighbors and those with vested interest in the status quo. However, the committed innovators or initial adopters of a new way are observed and even regarded silently as positive "reference others" by some community members, and their eventual success acts as vicarious reinforcement for potential adopters who now more readily forsake tradition and defy negative sanction to model their behavior after these venturesome few.

Bandura's reasoned argument parallels Erasmus' belief and observation that individuals normally modify their behavior when their new frequency interpretations permit clear connections between an alternative form of action and a consequence more desirable than they could achieve previously.

The application of this humanistic-behavioral "model of man in change" in this and subsequent chapters should further clarify its nature and demonstrate its usefulness.

Migrant Ideology

Migrant ideology refers to the "cognitive model which the migrant holds as to the nature and goals of his migration" (Philpott 1970:11). Most Hayriye men initially regarded emigration to Europe as a temporary experience, after which they would return to the village. Their individual goals included finding good-paying jobs, satisfying work, and possibly learning new technical skills. Their familial goals consisted of accumulating enough capital to make life for their families economically secure in Hayriye. Once in Europe, however, these men were exposed to an efficacious set of references or models that corresponded to a new system of prestige and statuses. Consequently, many changed their goals.

For example, prior to their 1965 departure for West Germany, the first contingent of village workers was told that they could bring their wives with them. In fact, the architect and teacher encouraged them to do so, saying, among other things, that just as European women work and earn good money, so could their wives. However, every one of the married men (61 from Hayriye) refused. Their typical response was: "What business do our wives have there among infidels? Isn't it enough that we go away to work? Our wives will stay home where they belong!" For them, preserving their women at home was a matter of honor. To do otherwise would have meant a loss of prestige and status according to their village's traditional system of sociocultural values.

But when they got to West Germany, the men saw that women there were not confined to their homes, that they held good-paying jobs, and that Turkish couples who were both employed were able to accumulate savings almost twice as fast as a man could working alone. Many Hayriye men used the husbands of these employed women as models or as reference sets, and the significant amount of extra money that the wives produced acted as vicarious reinforcement for their special behavior. It strongly influenced many Hayriye men to change their traditional position. Within a year, they began sending for their wives. By 1976, almost two-thirds of Hayriye's 93 married emigrant workers belonging to the cooperative had their wives with them in West Germany, and most of these women were working.[4]

By acting this way, these men would have lost prestige in terms of the traditional rules of a now outmoded village value system, but they gained prestige and status in terms of a new, evolving system, whose basic components have been adopted from reference sets and models outside the village.

Historically, the peasants of Hayriye had had only limited exposure to Turkey's more modern, urban-industrial society. Theirs was a relatively "closed" community in which residents evaluated themselves and others in terms of a traditional-rural system of values and statuses. However, once the channels of travel and communication between their village and important regional, national, and international centers became established, the villagers' traditional prestige and status system lost its importance. Lacking a comprehensive and well-supported anti-materialistic philosophy of life (such as that possessed by the Old Order Amish), they soon began to abandon, even reject, their traditional standards and adopt those of the more modern, industrial society, whose members had now become their new reference sets.

Members of their new reference sets (e.g., European industrial workers and highly successful Turkish emigrant workers) become especially efficacious models because the reward (i.e., money) they receive for their employment behavior is a generalized reinforcer with an extremely high saturation level. Not only can money be exchanged for a wide variety of desirable goods and services, but its acquisition and expenditure contribute importantly to the achievement of prestige and status in Europe's and in modern Turkey's industrial, sociocultural system. Consequently, not only do new, lucrative employment roles become important to the former peasants, but by extension, the perceived lifestyles of those occupying these roles become important as well. Peasants learn what they can about these new lifestyles through a process of observation and vicarious reinforcement. When they see that their behavioral models are handsomely rewarded for their characteristic behaviors, the peasants themselves are rewarded, albeit vicariously, and consequently are encouraged to adopt the perceived modes of their references' behavior.

Before going abroad, the villagers' impressions of Germans were limited, but positive. They had heard good reports from previous Turkish emigrants, and they knew that Turkey and Germany had always been friends, even allies in World War I. When they first arrived in Germany, almost all Hayriye men took up residence in factory dormitories and spent most of their time with fellow villagers or with other emigrants from Turkey. They formed a subsociety whose members worked together, ate together, and celebrated Islamic and Turkish holidays together in a European-Christian land. In time, as they became more familiar with their surroundings and had their wives join them, many moved to more residential parts of their cities and became somewhat more integrated into the German sociocultural milieu.[5]

Despite the fact that these workers were not fully accepted by most Germans, in subsequent years when they returned to Hayriye to spend their vacations, they emitted flowing reports about their German hosts. They described Germans as industrious, ingenious, honest, and "clean people, who knew neither lies nor curses." In fact, because of their outstanding qualities, the workers credited Germans with being more Muslim than many actual Muslims were. The only criticism voiced by some workers had to do with freedom and openness of German women. On the whole, however, they depicted Germans as extremely positive reference sets and models for change.

Emigrant workers desiring to get pay increases, promotions, or special privileges (such as securing jobs for relatives back in the village) tended to conform to the standards of their superiors, whether they be German or Turkish. New migrants tend to conform to the standards of those who have gone before them and have succeeded or become acculturated. The first "successful" migrant workers used Germans as their reference sets; they adopted the German work ethic,[6] learned some German, and rose to some supervisory capacity. They often acted as foremen, passing directives from their German superiors down to their Turkish subordinates.

This system of modeling has implications for areas of life outside the factory as well. Migrant workers not only allow their wives to work, but adopt German dress patterns, material values, as well as recreational and consumption styles, such as drinking beer and eating pork which are both prohibited by Islam. In short, they have developed a propensity for a Western, urban life style.

By 1974, over 90% of those who had gone to West Germany were still working there, and although most had originally planned to return to Hayriye, only about eight had constructed new, more substantial homes in the village with their savings. The majority had begun investing in urban real estate in Inegöl, Bursa, and Istanbul.[7] Many began by purchasing a building plot; then, as their savings warranted, they initiated the construction of a multistory building, one level at a time. An ideal unit consists of three or four stories; the first being for a retail outlet and the others for apartments. The worker ultimately plans to reside in one apartment and either operate a store from the first level or rent it out along with the other apartments. In Turkey, the new homes and apartment houses built by migrant workers have come to be called "*Almanya evleri*" ("Houses of Germany").

Urban real estate has been the most popular investment for Turkey's emigrant workers generally (Keleş 1976). Given its hedge against inflation and the limited investment alternatives available, it cannot be regarded as an irrational choice. The ownership of real estate also permits the returnee and his family the opportunity to continue participating in a more modern, urban life style. It appears that well over half of those who emigrated from Hayriye will relocate in cities when they return to Turkey, even though many could live comfortably in the village.

Community Goals. Legally, emigration through Hayriye's development cooperative also involved the communal goal of paying remittances into a fund which would be used for general village improvement. Each villager sent abroad in 1965 had agreed to remit TL 5,000 (about $556) in installments of TL 250 (about $28) during his first two years in Europe.[8] Members of the 1972 contingent had agreed to remit TL 8,000 over the same time period. (In both cases there was an initial two-month grace period.) However, only a small number of the first émigrés met their obligations willingly. Despite the personal and familial gains that cooperative emigration had brought them, they were ready to evade their responsibility to the village community that was an integral part of their emigration agreement. As the the cooperative's organizer, Ahmet Ozkan commented, "Many of the cooperative members who went abroad pushed this obligation aside and began to forget the village. In Turkish there is a proverb that says, 'Call the bear uncle [mother's brother] until you get across the bridge.' That is what the villagers did. Before they went abroad they had gladly agreed to make payments into the cooperative to provide better economic opportunities for the whole village. However, once they got to Germany and began earning money, they acted like they didn't care." Only after the cooperative took legal action did these workers grudgingly meet this term of their contract. The cooperative's officers informed the Government Employment Service of their problem, and the government decided not to issue exit visas to those who failed to meet their obligations. This meant that workers coming back to Turkey on vacation would not be permitted to return to Germany until they paid the cooperative its due.[9]

Through legal means the cooperative has been able to accumulate a substantial amount of capital for village projects (see next chapter). It is apparent, however, that the goals of many Hayriye emigrants do not extend beyond the level of primary kin to the village as a whole.

Hayriye's experience with its Village Development Cooperative (VDC) has been general in Turkey. The Turkish social scientist, Abadan-Unat, concludes that many Turkish villagers used VDCs almost exclusively as administrative "pretext" organizations for the purpose of obtaining jobs abroad. Members looked upon the first obligatory installment to their

VDC as an "administrative bribe" and refused to make further payments (Abadan-Unat 1976:26). The findings of Renselaar, Penninx and Velzen, who studied the VDC program generally in Turkey and specifically in two of its villages, concur with Abadan-Unat's conclusions and parallel Hayriye's experience:

> Soon after its widely heralded beginnings the VDC program faltered because of an explosion of cooperatives. Many VDC's were founded by members whose primary concern was springing to the front of the Employment Service waiting list for foreign job recruitment. These were popularly dubbed "Almanya-Kooperatifi" (German Cooperatives) to prevent any mistake about the motivation of those involved [Renselaar and Velzen 1976:107].

> The highly touted Village Development Co-operative Program has largely foundered because members were more interested in going abroad than committing themselves to furthering cooperative goals [Penninx and Velzen 1976:292].

The behavior of these villagers becomes more understandable if we view each emigrant worker's total set of social relations as consisting of a series of semiautonomous social and moral fields, each of which possesses a different strength of moral obligation to social commitments (see Moore 1973; Simić 1975). Within this series, the field formed by close kinship ties is unique, because it has its own social rules and interpersonal commitments which are backed by the highest degree of moral obligation. However, once we move beyond relations with close kin, we enter different fields with different rules and much weaker moral support for social relations. In brief, the concept of semiautonomous social and moral fields suggests the existence of varying sets of standards governing the conduct of relationships within and without one's primary group of social identification.

The idea of a moral field was suggested to Simić by Edward Banfield (1958), who explained the low level of political organization and intracommunity participation in small, impoverished southern Italian communities by a hypothesis he labeled *amoral familism*. Banfield's hypothesis maintained that the people he studied acted *as if* they were following this rule: "Maximize the material, short-run advantage to the nuclear family; assume that all others will do likewise." One whose behavior is consistent with this rule is called an "amoral familist"—he acts without morality only in relation to persons outside his family. That is, his extrafamilial relations are instrumental and exploitive; they are conducted on an "amoral" basis.[10]

With respect to VDCs in Turkey, Penninx and Velzen's (1976:295) findings conform well to Banfield's hypothesis:

> Our intensive research in two villages indicates, moreover, that as soon as investments on something greater than a family scale are made, there is a distinct risk that long-standing conflicts of interest within village society will intrude upon the scene and effectively paralyze hopes of production.

Banfield listed a number of "logical implications" of the rule. The following appear to apply in large part to Hayriye as well as to other villages in Turkey:

> In a society of amoral familists, no one will further the interest of the group or community except as it is to his private advantage to do so [Banfield 1958:83-84].

> In a society of amoral familists, the claim of any person or institution to be inspired by zeal for public rather than private advantage will be regarded as fraud [ibid. p. 95].

Certainly, Faik Ertan's early efforts to organize former and present villagers for the good of Hayriye was met with suspicion and charges of disguised self-interest. Ozkan and Ertan experienced the same reaction from many villagers when they first tried to organize the cooperative.

> In a society of amoral familists, organization (i.e., deliberately concerted action) will be very difficult to achieve and maintain [ibid. p. 86].

> In a society of amoral familists, the law will be disregarded when there is no reason to fear punishment [ibid. p. 90].

Successful organizations on the village level require trust in nonrelatives and many small sacrifices with few material rewards. Consequently, they have been infrequently attempted, and less frequently achieved. Hayriye's VDC was launched primarily because two outsiders supplied most of the organizational energy, and the villagers could clearly perceive the individual material gain to result from their participation. However, many of these participants were willing to disregard their contractual obligations to the cooperative and to the village until they had reason to fear some punishment. Hence, they refused to pay into the cooperative's development fund until the government threatened not to renew their visas. Despite these similarities, however, there appear to be several major differences between Banfield's south Italian village and Hayriye. For one, general identification with the village seems stronger among Hayriye's people. They speak of their village with a great deal of pride, even though they might be reluctant to volunteer much time or material aid to village projects. Also, some villagers, such as a few of the wealthy leaders, the *ağa*s, have acted somewhat paternalistically as though the entire village constituted one of their strong moral fields. They have devoted time and energy to provide the village with needed leadership; they have helped the needy; and at least two *ağa*s, who were functioning as elected village chiefs, supported the establishment of the cooperative— an organization designed to improve the lot of most villagers. In addition, although most people often behave as though they are primarily and almost exclusively concerned with their own kin and self-interest, their primary moral field is greater than the nuclear family. It commonly includes members of one's kindred and occasionally very close neighbors.

In general, however, while successful emigrants support their families and other close relatives left behind in the village and would experience a deep sense of shame if they were assailed for not doing so, many view wider communal commitments as inconveniences which can be avoided without the penalty of seriously negative social sanctions. These problems notwithstanding, the cooperative was able to achieve some impressive results in village development. These and other consequences of emigration will be discussed in the next chapter.

NOTES

1. The term "man" is, of course, being used in its generic sense; it includes both men and women.

2. Kunkel (1970:23-24) has conveniently summarized those general propositions of the various learning theories that he believes have relevance for sociological analysis.

3. Coincidently, Muzafer Sherif, the social psychologist whose research and writing have contributed significantly to the development of reference group theory, is Turkish-American.

4. In 1972, 82% of the emigrant workers in West Germany from Turkey were married, and 46% of these had their wives with them. The vast majority of these married women—88%—were employed (Abadan-Unat 1976:10). Also in 1972, the average savings in West Germany of workers from Turkey was DM 2,700 for bachelors as compared to DM 5,475 for married men accompanied by their wives (Abadan-Unat *et al*. 1976: 395). DM 3.2225=$1.00 (1972).

5. For an interesting study of residential patterns and social segregation of Turkish workers in Cologne, see Clark (1957).

6. In a 1968 study in Turkey by Krane (1975), interviews were conducted with managers of 41 industrial plants which employed men who had returned to Turkey after having worked in Europe. Most of these managers (59%) said they preferred to hire such returnees, and almost half said noticeable differences in attitudes and work habits existed between employees who had worked abroad and those who had not. Many managers described the returnees as more productive, industrious, orderly, conscientious, and able to assume responsibility.

7. In an informative study of investment patterns among emigrant workers from Turkey's rural Boğazlıyan District, Penninx and Velzen (1976: 297) found that frequently "a migrant invests in such a way as to suggest his original plans might have been to return to his place of origin, but his ultimate decision is to start anew in a large town. Money goes in early years to buy heavy agricultural machinery or to repair or to build a home in the migrant's village, but in later years [it] is poured into preparation for an urban future."

8. In addition, each villager had to pay TL 20 into Hayriye's treasury to cover application expenses.

9. Ozkan states that the voluntary remittance rate of workers from surrounding villages who went abroad via the cooperative was somewhat better than that of Hayriye's own emigrant workers.

10. Methodologically, Banfield maintains that his hypothesis or theory can explain ("in the sense of making intelligible and predictable") much of the behavior in question without being contradicted by the facts at hand (1958:83). He does not claim, however, that the coincidence of facts and theory "proves" the latter. "The value of the hypothesis...does not depend upon the possibility of showing that all, or even any, of the people... consciously follow the rule ....For the hypothesis to be useful, it need only be shown that they act *as if* they follow the rule" (ibid. 103). In this study, I also adhere to Banfield's methodological point.

For critiques of Banfield's general analysis, see Cancian (1961) and Silverman (1968).

10
Emigration
and Beyond

Money, enthusiasm, and excitement were among the first consequences of the 1965 contingent's immigration to Germany. The successful experiences of those who had gone caused others to want to join them. Villagers came to regard travel to Europe as a new *rite de passage* —a rite of modernization. By 1975, an estimated 300 Hayriye villagers were in Europe. This number included practically all of the 100 men who had gone through the cooperative, about 60 of their wives, and 75 or so of their children. About 50 additional men secured jobs in Europe through other channels. Some had registered their names with the Turkish Employment Service, and after one to several years' wait were fortunate to receive the cherished call. Others had become impatient with official channels and went abroad on their own. They purchased expensive tourist visas, visited relatives and friends in Europe, and searched successfully for work. Among the most fortunate, were those who received a "nominative call." Most frequently, their fathers or brothers, who were already abroad, had won the confidence of their employers and had vouched for the ability, industry, and character of their sons or brothers still in the village. The employers then requested these people by name through the Turkish Employment Service.

In 1974, one elderly Hayriye male observed that the villagers' social and economic ties with Germany had become so close, that Germany was now their "city." "Formerly," he explained, "Inegöl was our city. We didn't even know where Germany was. But today, so many of our relatives and neighbors live there that it has become as familiar to us as the nearest Turkish town."

Household Reorganization

The emigration of adult males from Hayriye has frequently required those members of their families and households remaining in the village to alter their roles and work out new patterns of social organization. Generally, members of nuclear households initiate more changes than members of extended households. For instance, young sons in nuclear households find they must shoulder some of the responsibilities relinquished by their absent fathers. While in extended households, such responsibilities are usually taken on by other adult males.

The situation is somewhat similar for wives. Those remaining behind in extended families generally maintain their traditional positions and exhibit little role change; whereas in the case of nuclear families, wives often assume many male tasks, such as caring for livestock, working longer days in the fields, and making more of the family's economic decisions. Women over forty may even make an occasional trip to Inegöl to transact business in the weekly regional market. For younger women, however, such a trip is still not tolerated. Despite her expanded decision-making responsibilities, a young woman's authority is still subordinate to that of her absent husband or her husband's father or mother, if they reside in the village. Should anyone of them overrule her, she must humbly submit.

Data gathered by the female Turkish social scientist Yenisey in two villages in Turkey's Boğazlıyan District parallel my observations in Hayriye. For example, in her sample of 49 nuclear families from which the husband had emigrated abroad, the "primary decision-maker" most frequently became the migrant's wife (69%), followed by the migrant's father (14%), his mother (10%), his brother (2%), and other males (4%). By contrast, in her sample of 93 extended households, the primary decision-maker was most frequently reported to be the migrant's father (41%), followed by the migrant's mother (27%), his wife (25%), his brother (3%), and other males (4%) (Yenisey 1976:334).

Yenisey's (1976:343) comments concerning village women who had experienced life in Europe are especially interesting. She observed that:

The few women from villages who stay for any real length of time in Europe and work display changes in thinking and attitudes when they come home. Returned female workers resent the lack of freedom in dress and in conduct they find in rural Turkey. Those living in Boğazlıyan town continue wearing their European apparel to some extent, but elsewhere they revert to traditional attire. Social control and gossip are things they all mention as very annoying, but they noticeably avoid trying to provoke talk about themselves. Also, although there seems to be much cooperation between husbands and wives who both are employed abroad as long as they remain abroad, cooperation in house-work and childcare, upon return women are likely to find their helpmates less supportive. Working women do shopping in Europe but back again in their villages, they must cede the task to men, unless they have returned to a nuclear family and their husbands have remained abroad. Certain women confided they now found the companionship of village women no longer enjoyable. They missed weekends in Europe when they could go sight-seeing, shopping, or visiting friends with their husbands. A husband and wife on the town together is a rare occurance [sic] in Boğazlıyan.

Hayriye villagers believe it highly unlikely that husbands and wives now working in Europe will resettle in the village. Their belief conforms to our "model of man in change." In such cases, both husband and wife would have been exposed to and subsequently would have adopted efficacious reference sets and models whose life styles have no possibility in a Turkish village. Consequently, they will attempt to maintain some sociocultural continuity by eventually relocating in a large city.

The following three cases from Hayriye demonstrate many of the changes an emigrant's village household must undergo in his absence.

Case 1: Ahmet's family. Ahmet went to Germany with the first village contingent in 1965 and received a position in a Volkswagen factory. He worked hard, established good relations with his German foreman, and successively managed to get jobs in the same plant for his 24-, 20-, and 17-year-old sons. The four men live together in a rented apartment with the oldest son's wife, a young woman from Hayriye, who keeps house for them. Ahmet's wife, his 18-year-old daughter, and his 9-year-old son continue to live in the village with Ahmet's aging father. They maintain themselves in Hayriye by growing enough food and keeping sufficient animals to meet household needs. They also engage in silk worm production to earn a small cash income. The strategy of this and many other families in Hayriye is to support themselves at home so that money earned in Germany can accumulate undisturbed.

Ahmet plans to work in Germany for a minimum of 15 years. By then his father will be too old to work the land so his entire extended family will most probably relocate in Inegöl. Ahmet's second and third sons will eventually marry. Having acquired technical skills in Germany, they will most likely resettle in one of Turkey's major industrial cities rather than return to live in the village. Consequently, they will all become permanent removals from Hayriye.

Case 2: Enver's family. Enver also went to Germany through the cooperative in 1965. His oldest son joined him in 1972. Enver's wife, two sons, and a daughter remain in the village where they keep a few chickens and cows and grow enough food to feed themselves throughout much of the year. The wife effectively manages the family's village affairs, but her 15-year-old son is developing into the "man of the house". Like other boys whose fathers and older brothers had gone abroad, he found himself shouldering new responsibilities. He provides his mother with male protection whenever she must venture into public places; he is in charge of the family's livestock, and he has taken over much of the field work.

With his savings Enver has already purchased two parcels of land in Bursa. On one he plans to put up an apartment building to house his family and earn rental income. On the other he is thinking of having a small textile plant constructed. He dreams of eventually leaving Germany with a pension, settling with his family in Bursa, and operating his own plant. Meanwhile, his once picturesque village home, the loyal victim of new aspirations, is deteriorating from years of neglect.

Case 3: Asim's family. Asim is the patriarch of a traditional, patrilocal extended family. Prior to 1965 his three sons lived at home. His oldest son was married and had two daughters. Asim's only daughter was also married, and resided in Bursa with her own family. When the village cooperative was formed, the men of Asim's household decided that the two bachelor sons would go to Germany, while the oldest would remain home.

The sons have worked in Germany continuously ever since, visiting the village only every other summer when they can spend their two-month accumulated vacation with relatives and friends. During one of these summer vacations, the older son eloped with a village girl against the wishes of both sets of parents. However, because the girl was 18, the elders could not legally prevent their marriage, which took place in Istanbul. The young bride accompanied her husband to Germany, and over the next three years she bore a boy and then a girl. When the girl reached two years of age, the couple decided to place the children in the care of relatives so that they both could work full-time. On their subsequent visit to Turkey their daughter became part of Asim's household in Hayriye, and their son joined the Bursa household of Asim's married daughter.

Meanwhile, Asim's youngest son also had his eye on a particular village girl, and asked his parents to arrange a marriage which could be consumated on his next vacation. But the desired girl belonged to a household already fragmented by emigration. Although only 17 years old, she was the woman of the house, as her mother was deceased and her older sister-in-law was in Germany with her married brother. Her father explained that she was desperately needed at home to care for him and her two younger siblings. He agreed to an engagement, but said a wedding would have to wait at least a year or two. Asim appreciated his neighbor's situation and arranged the engagement for his son's next home visit.

Trouble developed the following year however, when the engaged son returned again to the village, this time to take his bride. The situation in his fiancée's household had not changed, and her father wanted them to wait yet another year. Already impatient with delays, the young man threatened to elope, asserting that his fiancée had reached 18 and could marry of her own volition. Confronted with the potential disruption of interfamilial relations that passionate, youthful behavior can create, the elders agreed to the marriage on the condition that the girl remain in her natal household and not join her husband in Germany for at least one year. Reluctantly, Asim's son accepted the condition, and at summer's end he returned to his German bachelor's quarters a married, but still solitary man.

Since 1965 Asim has been maintaining a household and working a large farm with his wife, his eldest son, and that son's spouse and growing children. Despite access to his sons' European incomes, his household still maintains a high degree of self-sufficiency in the village by growing much of its own food and earning money from the sale of chestnuts, apples, and silk cocoons.

Although future plans are not definite, in all likelihood Asim's oldest son, a rustic man who has never spent any significant amount of time away from the village, will live out his life in Hayriye working the paternal lands. The sons currently in Germany will most probably opt for a continuation of their present urban-industrial lifestyle when they eventually return to Turkey.

These three cases are fairly representative of the types of rearrangements that many households have made. Asim's case is among the most complex; it involves the separation of parents from young children, the separation of young siblings from each other, the separation of a newly married couple, and the general fragmentation of a large extended household. Significantly, the existing kinship system with its role diffuseness, role flexibility, and ease of fosterage appears capable of accommodating, even supporting the hitherto unusual social arrangements resulting from large scale emigration.

Material and Economic Change

Prior to the 1965 emigration, the majority of Hayriye's poorer families were in debt. In addition, most men borrowed money to get to Germany. Hence, many early emigrants used a large part of their initial earnings to free themselves from old obligations. Thereafter, they began to indulge in Europe's consumer market, as well as save for their eventual return. When they visited the village on their annual or biannual vacations, they brought back the wonders of Europe. Some even drove home in their own merchandise-laden cars. Consequently, by the late 1960s, items of affluence began to adorn village homes. First came transistor radios, cassette tape recorders and sewing machines. Then came refrigerators and, more recently, television sets. (The village had two in the summer of 1974.) Furthermore, some villagers, especially younger males, began to adorn themselves with European clothes and watches. Whereas in the past Hayriye people carefully avoided ostentatious display because they feared others' envy and the evil eye, more recently they have been tending toward conspicuous show. This mode of prestige achievement so common in the West is being adopted by many village emigrants and their families.

In the days prior to emigration, villagers produced most of the items they consumed. But today they buy much of their clothing and all of their furniture ready-made from either Inegöl, Bursa, or Europe. Even bread is imported daily and sold in the Cooperative Store.

Presently, villagers still grow most of their own food, but agricultural production has decreased markedly. Although foreign earnings purchased Hayriye's first two tractors, villagers work only about one-third the land they formerly did and let the remainder lie fallow. Their oxen have dwindled from eighty pairs to thirty. Many of the remaining village men are elderly and can now afford not to work the exhaustingly hilly terrain. But hiring laborers is almost impossible. From 1965 to 1974 a farm worker's daily wage had grown seven-fold, reaching TL 35-40 for a woman and TL 70-75 for a man. Despite these increases, the villagers have no one to hire. Emigration and more attractive work alternatives, such as hauling logs for the Forestry Service at TL 100-150 a day, have diverted many men from the soil. The situation has given rise to a standard village joke. As the village's active farmers pass the central tea garden where their elderly friends— mostly the fathers of emigrants—are sitting and enjoying a drink along with the warm rays of the sun, the farmers call out, "Hello my lords. Do you have marks? You do! Then all is just fine!"

Almost all threshing is now done by machine, and men rarely engage in the traditional exchange of work (*nadi*). The custom survives, however, among women.

Village Development Projects

From the beginning, much of the cooperative's direction and energy have emanated from Ahmet Ozkan and Faik Ertan—two "outsiders." They have continuously advised the cooperative's members on investments and have helped plan specific projects. By 1967 the cooperative had accumulated a sizable development fund from workers' remittances, and one of its first investment projects was the establishment of a cooperative general store which employs a full-time operator. The store offers the villagers a wider variety of items than do Hayriye's two other stores, and it has been instrumental in keeping prices down. Anyone can buy there, but only cooperative members can maintain credit accounts. The store turns its profits back into the cooperative.

In 1967 the cooperative also decided to enter the poultry business by investing in a modern chicken and egg production project. It had a poultry house constructed and hired a villager, who was then instructed in modern poultry production techniques, to operate the enterprise full-time. The project is scaled to about 1,500 chickens and utilizes commercial feeds. Income from sales, made mostly in Inegöl, have resulted in small profits, which revert to the cooperative. More recently, in 1974-75, Ahmet has been encouraging cooperative members to launch a modern livestock project, which would initially involve 50 head of quality cattle. This project appears to be highly practical, given the village's increased amount of fallow land which could profitably be used for grazing.

The cooperative also facilitated the movement of people and goods between Hayriye and Inegöl by purchasing a four-wheel drive jeep truck in 1970. A full-time driver was hired to operate and maintain the vehicle which normally transports about a dozen villagers and their bundles into the city every morning and brings them back in the late afternoon. On Thursday, the weekly market day, the driver makes several round trips to accommodate the larger number of people desiring to do business in town. The jeep also carries mail and merchandise for the cooperative store. In 1974, the one-way fare of TL 5 per person equaled the fare of the early 1960s, when privately owned vehicles from outside Hayriye provided transportation.

In addition to these cooperative projects, Hayriye has profited from the earnings of its approximately 200 European employees in other ways. For example, during the early 1970s, village leaders collected contributions from practically all Hayriye households to help the village finance the construction of a new bridge linking two of its quarters. In the same manner, money was gathered to help secure power lines for the village, which got electricity for the first time in 1973. Significantly, in both cases, contributors benefited directly from the projects they supported.

Many villagers speak of these accomplishments with undisguised pride and attribute them to the cooperative and Ahmet Ozkan's leadership. Yet, these same villagers often exhibit little or no *active* interest in the cooperative's on-going business. The general meeting called in the summer of 1974 provides a typical illustration. Of the over 250 members and their representatives (fathers and relatives of those working in Europe), only a handful attended. Consequently, the meeting had to be postponed.[1]

Villagers and European workers have also shown that there are definite limits beyond which they will not support communal projects. For instance, in 1973 Ozkan convinced a government agency to offer Hayriye a small fruit and vegtable canning factory if the villagers would provide the necessary site for the plant and promise to operate it. In return, the plant would employ several villagers full-time and offer everyone the opportunity to can his produce in the area's first modern facility for either home consumption or sale. Ozkan helped arrange a meeting in Hayriye so that a government representative could explain the project to the villagers. But, only five men showed up, and no one was willing to provide the necessary land. Hence, the plant was offered to another village, which accepted it immediately.

Probably sensing the centrifugal consequences that emigration and affluence were having for Hayriye, and fearing that an idea implemented to save the community was contributing more to its dissolution, Ozkan devised a scheme he hoped would ignite new interest in the village. He drew up architectural plans for a modern, multipurpose building to be located in Hayriye's center. It would contain a small cinema, the general store, a post office, and rooms for guests, the village chief, a library, a coffeehouse, and a first aid station. In the winter of 1973-74 he presented his drawings and ideas to the villagers assembled in one of Hayriye's coffeehouses. Ozkan depicted the proposed building as a communal center for social, cultural, governmental, and economic activity. Its facilities and conveniences would draw everyone. More important, probably, it would make Hayriye more attractive to villagers currently working in Europe. By donating his own time and utilizing his contacts in the construction industry, he estimated the building would cost a low TL 350,000 (about $25,000). The money, he hoped, would be contributed by Hayriye's European employees and others interested in the village's future.

That same winter Ozkan traveled to Europe to discuss his plan personally with Hayriye's emigrants and ask for their monetary support. But he was met with little enthusiasm. By summer he had collected less than TL 20,000 (about $1,430), and it now appears that the community center may never be more than a dream. For many Hayriye people, communal goals and commitments remain in a weak moral field.

In the village coffeehouses some men complained to me about Ozkan's disappointment. They reasoned that he had achieved so much for Hayriye, that villagers should feel obliged to follow his advice and support his new projects. They accused fellow villagers of showing gratitude in words, not in deeds. Others also sympathized with Ozkan, but perceived the eventual exodus from Hayriye of many who can afford to go as a basic reason for communal disinterest. Ironically, those who can now leave the village are the ones who have profited from the cooperative and are especially needed to support communal endeavors.

Economic Stratification

Practically all Hayriye households have materially profited, either directly or indirectly, from emigration. With respect to economic stratification, emigration has had an elevating effect for households in the middle and lower strata. Table 13 demonstrates this change by illustrating the village's indigenous system of tax (*salma*) ranking at two different time periods: 1961 (four years before the first group emigration) and 1975. As explained previously, every year the village chief and Council of Elders assign each household to one of seven tax ranks on the basis of its estimated wealth *in the village*. They consider such items as the value of a household's homestead, land, animals and farm equipment. They do not consider external wealth, such as urban real estate and savings accounts. Consequently, many households were much wealthier in 1975 than their tax ranks indicated.

Table 13
1961 and 1975 Tax (*Salma*) Rankings
of Hayriye Households

Tax Rank	1961 Households				1975 Households			
	N.	%			N.	%		
1	8	4.5			8	4.8		
2	9	5.1			23	13.9		
3	30	16.9	}	43.3	31	18.8	}	62.4
4	47	26.4			72	43.6		
5	51	28.7	}	47.2	14	8.5	}	18.8
6	27	15.2			17	10.3		
7	6	3.3			0	0.0		
TOTALS	178	100.1			165	99.9		

Over the fourteen years between 1961 and 1975 few, if any, households fell to lower tax ranks. Emigration has generally reduced the range of disparity between the richest and poorest households and created a predominant clustering of households in the middle economic ranks. By 1975, the impoverished seventh rank had been eliminated completely.

These modifications in the economic stratification system are associated with changes in the mode of interpersonal relations. For example, many Hayriye residents complained to me that their former neighbors who emigrated to Germany have taken on new airs. "Formerly they were peasants like us. Now they've gone to Germany and think they're aristocracy. But what are they there? Only factory workers!"

The money in-flow has also affected relations between the old rich and the formerly poor. One old village *ağa* commented as follows: "Previously, there would be three or four people waiting for me outside my gate every morning. They came to ask for either corn, wheat, money, or work. I helped them as much as I could. Now, many of these same people act as if they don't recognize me."

In addition, many elderly village men attribute the increased economic independence of the young to the latter's tendency to be disrespectful. The following incident, which I observed in 1972, was classified by villagers as just one example of what they regard as a serious social problem.

The village's jeep pickup carries from 10 to 12 passengers in its enclosed back and two or a very tight three passengers up front with the driver. The seats in the cabin are preferred because they are more comfortable than the back benches and offer a clear view. One particular day when I was boarding the jeep for a ride into Inegöl, a competition developed for the front seat between several elderly men and a man in his twenties. The young man had gotten into the seat and refused to give way to anyone else. One of the elderly villagers argued that the front seat should be reserved for women, the elderly, and the sick. In reply, the young man, who was neatly dressed in an urban suit, countered that anyone who pays his fare has an equal right to the front. "First come, first served." "No, no," the elderly villager countered. "Your attitude is wrong. It lacks humanity. In all civilized nations of the world, special consideration is rendered to the sick, elderly, lame, and expectant women." Unconvinced, the young man looked away in silent disagreement and continued to occupy his place.

NOTE

1. Eramus (1961:86-87) notes that formalizing cooperative action among peasants is not always as natural as many idealistic planners believe. He observed that:

> Nearly all the work and production cooperatives organized by Haitian extension agents as a means of introducing changes eventually failed. They ended when the agent was moved to a new locale, when jealousies sprang up among members, or when members failed to do their duties....Each venture, in a way, was like a small messianic

movement led by an inspired idealist; and each was consequently very much dependent upon the personal qualities of the particular extension agent and the rapport he was able to establish between himself and the peasantry. A change of extension agents...ended in the collapse of the "cooperative."

Hence, it appears that in Haiti, as in Hayriye, the success of a local village cooperative depends largely on the personalities and energy of outside organizers and directors.

11
Overview
and Conclusion

Since the early 1960s, an asymetrical relationship has characterized interactions between the highly industrialized "center" countries of Western Europe (especially West Germany) and the "periphery" countries of Southern Europe and the Mediterranean. Whereas the center countries are the loci of highly advanced technologies, expanding economies, and affluent living standards, the less industrialized periphery countries with their lower living standards constitute industrial markets and sources of raw materials as well as cheap export labor.[1]

The center has developed a special value system which supports and promotes its Western, urban-industrial society. Within this system, concepts such as productivity, expansion, export surplus, along with conspicuous production, acquisition, display, and consumption constitute core values. The center's institutions not only thrive on these values, but radiate them, for the center has a built-in need to expand. The more far-reaching its domain, the more successful its promoters. In the past, most peoples of the periphery articulated with the center only occasionally and fragmentarily. However, as a result of technological advances in transportation and communication and international migration, articulation has become more regular and integrated. Peoples of the periphery articulate not merely through the mediated message, but through the adoption of reference sets, groups, and persons as well as through a system of direct and vicarious reinforcement. The monetary rewards for adherence to center norms are generalized reinforcers whose satiation boundaries are practically limitless. The system's stimuli are human motivations for material abundance and the social prestige that such abundance symbolizes.

For decades previous to the 1960s, a similar asymmetrical relationship existed within the peripheral countries themselves between urban and rural areas. In essence, their cities acted as the initial receptors and transmitters of Western industrial civilization. As a consequence, millions of peasants abandoned their villages in favor of these cities, having been attracted by perceived urban opportunities and repulsed by limited rural possibilities. More often than not, however, their aspirations of acquiring an idealized urban lifestyle have gone unfulfilled, and the initial impact of their imigration has been the partial peasantization of cities.

For Turkey, the 1950-1970 period was one of exceptional socio-cultural and economic change. The country experienced a population boom; the mechanization of agriculture displaced rural workers and their families; large investments in highway and transportation systems facilitated rapid, but premature urbanization. Rural-urban migration caused the number of cities with populations of 100,000 or more to increase from five in 1950 to twenty in 1970, and it is expected that by 1985 their number will reach 52 (Keleş 1972:2). During the same 1950-1970 period, the populations of five major cities (Istanbul, Ankara, Izmir, Adana, and Bursa) more than doubled, with Ankara quadrupling. Because Turkey's rate of urbanization greatly exceeds her rate of industrialization, large scale urban migration has led to social and economic imbalances in cities, which are increasingly ringed by migrant shanty towns. By 1960, Turkey was faced with high unemployment and a serious balance of payments deficit.

By contrast, during the 1950s West Germany's declining birth rate, her top-heavy age pyramid, and her highly skilled population combined with an enormous economic expansion to create a need for foreign workers to fill the many job openings in industry that required little or no skill. Until the construction of the Berlin Wall in 1961, West Germany had conveniently absorbed refugee labor from East Germany. Thereafter, however, she became increasingly dependent on other countries for workers. In the early 1960s it certainly appeared as though West Germany and other center countries were rescuing peripheral countries, like Turkey, when the former agreed to import and employ the latter's excess labor. The resulting international migration enabled many people from Turkey's rural communities to by-pass their own major cities, cross national boundaries, and become intimately associated with the center.

On the level of the individual worker, the economic consequences of labor emigration appear quite positive. Those who left Turkey for Western Europe generally earn ten to seventy times more than they could have if they had remained, and the vast majority of returnees claim emigration was a beneficial experience. In fact, German surveys show that most foreign workers want to remain in the host country longer than the time periods stated in their contracts. Many of those who have successfully worked and saved in Western Europe express discontent when they return to Turkey. According to a 1974 Turkish State Planning Organization report, 78.2% of those workers surveyed who had returned permanently to Turkey from Europe expressed serious dissatisfaction with economic opportunities in their home country and wished to reemigrate (Kiray 1976:234). Yet, we must be concerned with the extensive family fragmentation that emigration has caused and with the possible negative consequences that absent parents and a series of foster homes may have on the personality development of Turkish children.

The managers of German firms also appear basically satisfied with imported labor. Despite the significant cost of hiring foreign workers (in terms of government and transportation fees, training and housing expenses, etc.), their numbers have increased over the years substantially. Hence, it may be assumed that employing foreigners has been less costly than the alternatives of hiring Germans or investing in labor-saving capital equipment.

As we move above the levels of the individual Turkish worker and the German firm, however, the economic picture is less clear. Some researchers believe temporary emigration provides Turkey with a degree of relief from high unemployment, adds significantly to foreign exchange reserves through remittances, and presents Turkey with an excellent opportunity to develop a sizable proportion of its own industrial labor force more efficiently than it could if it were training workers domestically. Other researchers counter that emigration is draining Turkey of its skilled human resources, because the average education of its emigrants is higher than that of their nonmigrating cohort group, and a high proportion of emigrants already possessed industrial or craft skills needed at home.[2] Moreover, Turkey has become ominously dependent on workers' remittances, which now constitute its largest single foreign exchange earner. In 1972, for instance, remittances were equal to 83.6 percent of all other exports combined. Instead of applying these foreign earnings to the creation of future employment opportunities at home for workers who must eventually return from Europe, Turkey has been using them primarily to pay for increasingly large import bills. Unfortunately, the Turks' living experience in Europe and the large volume of European imports are contributing to a disdain for domestic products and a preference for foreign goods that will most likely worsen Turkey's already precarious balance of payments problem. Despite the fact that high population growth rates have contributed to Turkey's urbanization and unemployment problems in the past, Turkey's population continues to increase unchecked at about 2.5 percent per year. In addition, Turkey's unemployment has doubled since 1965, even though about three-quarter million Turkish citizens emigrated to Europe during this period.

It appears that Turkey has been complacently growing more and more dependent on a relatively insecure means of economic vitality, when it should regard international migration as merely a temporary grace period during which it must vigorously address its own internal structural problems of rapid urbanization, population growth, inflation, unemployment, social fragmentation, and balance of payments deficits. Unfortunately, it seems that the implementation of a rational plan of national development which does not rely heavily on remittances is not imminent.

This book has concerned itself primarily with the consequences of emigration (or the center-periphery association) for one particular village, and through the careful analysis of this case it has attempted to contribute generally to an understanding of the sociocultural and economic changes involved. At this point, it would be useful to recap Hayriye's experience in light of the "model of man in change" and other constructs discussed in Chapter IX.

If we begin by following Erasmus' (1961) advice and focus on prestige motivation as the main stimulus to cultural change, we will see that prestige motivation takes on different forms under diverse economic and social conditions. Prior to the 1965 large scale migration from Hayriye to Europe, the village was an agrarian peasant community structured by a plow technology, a simple division of labor, a kinship-based social system, a narrow range of consumer goods, and a near-subsistence economy. Peasant households formed productive and consumptive units, producing most of the goods they consumed.

The range of moral fields in which people manifested strong, moral commitments to others was quite narrow, usually being confined to members of households or limited kindreds. Villagers cooperated with their kin and members of tight neighborhood groups for their mutual benefit. Because most residents were largely confined to their remote village and were embedded in its network of social relations, their "reference others" and models for behavior consisted primarily of local people. The rewards for appropriate behavior were locally dispensed in the form of social acceptance.

In order to avoid invidious sanction in the form of gossip, envy, and the evil eye, villagers commonly hid any surplus or special items they accumulated rather than display them. Those wealthy few who owned large amounts of land and could accumulate sizable surpluses were socially and religiously obligated to conspicuously share part of their wealth in the form of large contributions to the maintenance of the mosque and school, meat and grain to the poor on religious holidays, and other material aid to general village projects and the needy. In return, villagers granted these men special prestige, leadership status, and the title *ağa*. But should a wealthy man not distribute a sizable portion of his surplus, the villagers would make him the object of their invidious sanction.

A few paternalistic *ağa*s acted as if they regarded the entire village as one of their strong moral fields, and by so doing they provided some cohesion to a settlement atomized by the many separate kin groups that formed a series of discrete moral fields. These *ağa*s did not behave this way because they were necessarily benevolent or altruistic (although some may have been both). They acted paternalistically toward the village because of an historic, religiously sanctioned tradition reinforced by strong local pressures to share and their own desire for special prestige. The recipients of an *ağa*'s distribution did not regard the act as charity, for they considered it his moral obligation to share. They compensated him with prestige and felt they were instrumental in helping him earn grace (*sevap*) in the eyes of Allah.

Because villagers value their independence highly (whether such independence be fact or fiction), a leader's ability to direct them depended principally on persuasion, and his persuasive powers rested mainly on his reputation for sharing. Under these conditions, common villagers exercised some control over the distribution of an *ağa*'s surplus.

Among the many factors transfiguring this traditional situation, large scale migration to Europe has been the most significant. Migration created the conditions necessary for the effective emulation of models or "reference others" whose characteristic life styles had no functional relationship to Hayriye. Lucrative foreign earnings —the rewards of their newly adopted behavior modes—are enabling former Hayriye peasants to relocate in cities and attempt to pursue a more modern, urban way of life. The money flow back into the village has freed many families from dependence on the soil and has obliterated traditional economic and prestige dependencies between rich and poor. Foreign earnings have improved the financial situations of practically all villagers who now increasingly participate in national and international commercial markets as consumers.

Formerly, village poverty, a near-subsistence economy, and invidious sanction conjointly limited conspicuous ownership and consumption. Now, under different conditions, more and more villagers are opting to enjoy newly available goods, and invidious sanction has lost its efficacy. Today, those villagers capable of the greatest displays of acquisition provoke emulation and enhance rather than diminish their prestige and influence.

On the international level, conspicuous production is a principal means of gaining prestige. Because the advanced, industrial countries of the center greatly outproduce those of the periphery and display much higher standards of living, they have become models of emulation. On the village level, the dominant consumption pattern had been modest and utilitarian. However, now that incomes significantly surpass the subsistence level, the villagers' desire to emulate urban models is pushing consumption towards "luxuries" and the purchase of new status symbols.

The anthropologist Brandes (1975) made observations similar to mine as he studied the impact of emigration on a village in Spain. He writes as follows:

> Villagers admit that their two worst vices are envy (*envidia*) and selfishness (*egoismo*). Extreme poverty and scarcity in the pueblos, they say, have always instilled a general fear of revealing one's possessions, lest one be forced into sharing with others more than one can reasonably afford, or one becomes the object of envy, scorn, and theft....Paradoxically, now that the village has prospered and there *are* valuable family possessions, people have become less concerned about revealing them. If anything, the more a family can surround itself with the symbols of urban life—radio, television, gas heater, fashionable clothing—the greater its prestige [Brandes 1975:185].

Economic leveling and a new value orientation have also undermined the traditional persuasive leadership roles of the village *ağa*s. As invidious emulation replaces invidious sanction, and as the material goods necessary for emulation originate externally, the *ağa*s can no longer earn prestige and leadership through conspicuous giving. Consequently, it now appears that the village lacks influential, indigenous leaders who regard all of Hayriye as a strong, unified moral field. Without the *ağa*s and the traditional socio-economic context, the village headship no longer carries the paternalistic and persuasive authority it once did. Hence, the village's atomization into discrete households and kin groups appears almost complete. Because each kin group is concerned primarily with its own welfare, and because the only role traditionally able to override this discreteness has been eliminated and not replaced by functional alternatives, we may conclude that in this one respect prosperity has weakened the village as a community.

What have been some of the other ways in which prosperity and mobility have affected Hayriye?

Emigration opportunities permitted many villagers (especially adult males) to explore new avenues for acquiring prestige. A variety of comparatively lucrative employment possibilities was presented to them, and they were exposed to new, more attractive ways of living. As they reoriented themselves to this new world, their village's traditional system of roles, statuses, and values lost its importance. For them, Hayriye has become a place of past identification, rather than a home community. They refer to it often, but return to it seldom. Together, they constitute a kind of dispersed identity group with a village of their past as a common reference point.

Even those remaining in the village have become externally oriented, as many of their relatives now live either in Turkish cities or in Europe and their sources of income and destinies lay beyond Hayriye. In 1974 practically all villagers I talked with said Hayriye's major needs were an improved road and a public telephone to connect it more closely with the outside.

In Hayriye, peasant agriculture based on human and animal power has become a low status occupation, which villagers no longer regard as a dignified way of life. The few young men who continue to work their fathers' lands in the traditional way are considered unattractive spouses by village girls, who prefer husbands that carry passports to Turkish cities or to Europe.

Some villagers have invested part of their families' foreign earnings in agricultural machinery and increasingly involve themselves in more capital-intensive cultivation. These we may call *postpeasants*. Others have chosen to abandon their marginal lands and engage in conspicuous leisure. Foreign earnings have brought a high degree of economic equality to Hayriye, as former peasants with insufficient land must no longer work for others. Hence, the traditionally wealthy have lost a source of cheap labor upon which they depended.

Today, Hayriye's inhabitants are mostly females, old men, and young boys. Its population profile displays a large gap in the male 20 to 50 age bracket, as migration has drawn away most of the men in this potentially most dynamic age group. As a result, many villagers comment that Hayriye is a less lively place than it once was (cf. Barrett 1974). The Hayriye folk dance group, which everyone had been so proud of, disbanded when practically all its members migrated to Europe. The village's only accordian players went too. Important village ritual, such as wedding celebrations, have been abbreviated so as to convenience city guests and people on the move. Villagers admit that weddings in Inegöl are now more enjoyable than those in Hayriye.

Migration and the influx of foreign ideas and products are also contributing to the gradual elimination of Hayriye as a distinctive Georgian community and subculture. Clothing, food, ritual, and language are all being modified or transformed by the majority Turkish culture. Many village homes are gradually falling into disrepair, as their inhabitants abandon them or plan to do so. This unique Georgian architecture is not brought to the cities, where buildings more reminiscent of concrete block houses become the dwellings of former villagers. A new *bagen* has not been constructed in Hayriye since sometime before the 1965 group emigration to Europe.

Hayriye's inhabitants are contending with at least two markedly different worlds. In 1975 I received a letter from Ahmet Ozkan which related how one of the village's former *ağas*—an elderly and pious man— had made the pilgrimage to Mecca with his matronly wife, and thereby achieved one of his last and greatest ambitions. After returning from this trip, the first major one of their lives, they decided to fly to Germany to visit their sons who worked and lived there. In terms of their own experience and in the eyes of fellow villagers, both trips were of great significance. They had pilgrimaged to the heart of Islam and to a center of the modern, industrial age. Having done so, the village community accorded them a combined increment of religious and social prestige that previously had not existed.

During the twentieth century, the combined processes of industrialization, urbanization, and migration have been depleting the world's treasury of distinctive peasant cultures. In Hayriye, the complex phenomenon of change derives its dynamics and direction from the aspirations and actions of numerous individuals whose life movements blend to create the images depicting Hayriye's story. These people have formed new perceptions and redesigned strategies to achieve new goals through the utilization of mobility channels and other available resources. Consequently, they have altered traditional kinship relations, friendship bonds, employment and investment options, and criteria for individual evaluation to varying degrees so as to accomplish the objectives comprising their modernizing lives.

Historically, peasant existence has been associated with low levels of consumption and resource utilization. Today, millions of peasants, like those of Hayriye, are abandoning their past and venturing into an urban, industrial future. Their former life style, however difficult, was a tested and proven means of survival with a long historical record of success; the majority of people who have ever inhabited this earth did so as peasants. Their new life option, urban, industrial civilization, is the latest development in mankind's campaign to conquer earth. Thrust forward by the dynamics of growth and expansion, it has attained centrality and dominance in our day. Yet, this dynamism, as we know it, has a comparatively short future. The natural resources upon which it is based are finite and many are close to exhaustion (see Meadows et al. 1974; Brown 1972).

Overcrowded cities, insufficiency of natural resources, increased industrial pollution of the natural environment, world food and energy shortages, inequalities in the distribution system, and other constraints on raising consumption standards will combine to prevent most aspiring people from achieving their ambitions of joining the cultural center of material prosperity. Instead, they may fall into the culture of discontent (Magnarella 1974:180ff).

This book is about people who appear to be making it. If so, they may be among the "fortunate" few. The salvation of mankind, however, will depend on those willing to remain behind and preserve a value system and life style consonant with the coming age of scarcity and conservation. Given the needs of the future, a variety of postpeasantries based on labor-intensive rather than capital-intensive farming will do much to reverse the trend toward industrialization and rapid natural resource depletion, and thereby provide mankind with the food and environment it needs to survive.

NOTES

1. According to official German statistics, as of January, 1973, the major labor exporting "periphery" countries had the following numbers of migrant workers employed in West Germany: Italy, 409,448; Greece, 268,408; Spain, 179,157; Portugal, 68,994; Yugoslavia, 465,611; and, Turkey, 528,414 (Abadan-Unat et al. 1976:387). I borrowed the "center" - "periphery" concepts from Shils (1961).

2. For a more detailed discussion of the German and Turkish experiences with labor migration, see Abadan-Unat et al. (1976) and the volume edited by Krane (1975).

References

Abadan-Unat, Nermin
    1974   "Turkish External Migration and Social Mobility." In *Turkey: Geographical and Social Perspectives*. Peter Benedict, *et al.*, Eds. Leiden: E.J. Brill. pp. 362-402.
    1976   "Turkish Migration to Europe (1960-1975)." In *Turkish Workers in Europe 1960-1975*. Nermin Abadan-Unat, *et al.*, Leiden: E. J. Brill. pp. 1-44.

Abadan-Unat, Nermin, *et al.*
    1976   *Turkish Workers in Europe 1960-1975*. Leiden: E.J. Brill.

Alder, Alfred
    1956   *The Individual Psychology of Alfred Adler*. H.L. Ansbacher and R.R.Ansbacher, Eds. New York: Basic Books.

Allen, W.E.D.
    1932   *A History of the Georgian People*. New York: Barnes and Noble.

Alpat, Sabahattin
    1969   "Critical Review of Demographic Data Obtained by
                Turkish Population Census." In *Turkish Demography*.
                F.C. Shorter and B. Güvenç, Eds. Ankara: Hacettepe
                University Pub. No. 7. pp. 43-63.
Antoun, Richard T.
    1972   *Arab Village.* Bloomington, Indiana: Indiana University
                Press.
Arberry, Arthur J. (Translator)
    1955   *The Koran Interpreted.* Volume II. Toronto: Macmillan
                Co.
Bandura, Albert
    1969   *Principles of Behavior Modification.* New York: Holt,
                Rinehart and Winston.
Bandura, Albert, and Richard H. Walters
    1963   *Social Learning and Personality Development.* New
                York: Holt, Rinehart and Winston.
Banfield, Edward C.
    1958   *The Moral Basis of a Backward Society.* New York:
                The Free Press.
Barrett, Richard A.
    1974   *Benabarre: The Modernization of a Spanish Village.*
                New York: Holt, Rinehart and Winston.
Bayri, Mehmet Halit
    1947   *Istanbul Folkloru.* Istanbul: Turk Yayınevi.
Bertalanffy, Ludwig von
    1968   *General System Theory.* New York: George Braziller.
Brandes, Stanley H.
    1975   *Migration, Kinship, and Community: Tradition and
                Transition in a Spanish Village.* New York: Academic
                Press.
Brown, Lester R.
    1972   *World without Borders.* New York: Random House.
Bursa Il Yıllığı/1967
    1968   *Istanbul:* Fono Matbaası.
Cancian, Frank
    1961   "The Southern Italian Peasant: World View and Political
                Behavior." *Anthropological Quarterly* 34:1:1-18.
Cardona, Ramiro, and Alan Simmons
    1975   "Toward a Model of Migration in Latin America." In
                Migration and Urbanization. B.M. du Toit and H.I. Safa,
                Eds. The Hague: Mouton. pp. 19-48

Catford, J.C.
1977   "Mountain of Tongues: The Languages of the Caucasus."
                Annual Review of Anthropology 6:283-314.
Clark, John R.
1975   "Residential Patterns and Social Integration of Turks
                in Cologne." In *Manpower Mobility across Cultural
                Boundaries.* R.E. Krane, Ed. Leiden: E.J. Brill. pp. 61-76.
Cohen, Erik
1977   "Recent Anthropological Studies of Middle Eastern
                Communities and Ethnic Groups." *Annual Review of
                Anthropology* 6:315-347.
Dalton, George
1974   "How Exactly Are Peasants 'Exploited'?" *American
                Anthropologist* 76:3:553-561.
Dersimi, M. Nuri
1952   *Kürdistan Tarihinde Dersim.* Aleppo: Ani Matbassı.
De Vos, George
1975   "Ethnic Pluralism: Conflict and Accommodation." In
                Ethnic Identity: Cultural Continuities and Change. G.
                De Vos and L. Romanucci-Ross, Eds. Palo Alto, Calif.:
                Mayfield. pp. 1-41.
du Toit, Brian M.
1975   "A Decision-Making Model for the Study of Migration."
                In *Migration and Urbanization.* B.M. du Toit and H.I.
                Safa, Eds. The Hague: Mouton. pp. 49-76.
Dodd, C.H.
1969   *Politics and Government in Turkey.* Berkeley and Los
                Angeles: University of California Press.
Donaldson, Bess Allen
1938   *The Wild Rue: A Study of Muhammadan Magic and
                Folklore in Iran.* London: Luzac.
el-Zein, Abdul Hamid
1977   "Beyond Ideology and Theology: The Search for the
                Anthropology of Islam." *Annual Review of Anthro-
                pology* 6:227-254.
Erasmus, Charles J.
1961   *Man Takes Control.* Minneapolis: University of
                Minnesota Press.
Fernea, Robert A.
1970   *Shaykh and Effendi.* Cambridge, MA: Harvard
                University Press.
Form, William H. and James A. Geschwender

1962   "Social Reference Basis of Job Satisfaction: The Case of
                Manual Workers." *American Sociological Review*
                27:2:228-237.
Foster, George M.
    1962   *Traditional Cultures and the Impact of Technological
                Change.* New York: Harper and Row.
    1967   *Tzintzuntzan: Mexican Peasants in a Changing World.*
                Boston: Little Brown and Co.
Frey, Frederick W.
    1964   "Education: Turkey." In *Political Modernization in
                Japan and Turkey.* R.E. Ward and D.A. Rustow, Eds.
                Princeton: Princeton University Press. pp. 205-235.
Frey, Frederick W., and Leslie L. Ross
    1967   "Social Structure and Community Development in
                Rural Turkey: Village and Elite Leadership Relations."
                Rural Development Research Project Report No. 10.
                Cambridge, MA: Massachusetts Institute of Technology.

Gamkrelidze, Th. V., and T.E. Gudava
    1974   "Caucasian Languages." *Encyclopaedia Britannica.*
                Macropaedia 3:1011-15.

Gamst, Frederick C.
    1974   *Peasants in Complex Society.* New York: Holt,
                Rinehart and Winston.
Geertz, Clifford
    1962   "Studies in Peasant Life: Community and Society."
                In *Biennial Review of Anthropology 1961.* B. Siegel, Ed.
                Stanford, Calif.: Stanford University Press. pp.1-41.
    1973   *The Interpretation of Cultures.* New York: Basic Books.
Geiger, Bernhard, *et al.*
    1956   *The Caucasus.* Volumes I and II. New Haven, Conn.:
                Human Relations Area Files.
Genel Nüfus Sayımı 1965
    1969   Ankara: State Institute of Statistics.
Gibb, H.A.R., and J.H. Kramers, Eds.
    1953   *Shorter Encyclopaedia of Islam.* Leiden: E.J. Brill.
Grigolia, Alexander
    1939   *Custom and Justice in the Caucasus: The Georgian
                Highlanders.* Ph. D. dissertation. University of
                Pennsylvania.

Halasi-Kun, T.
1956   "Historical Setting." In *The Caucasus*. Volume I. Bernard
            Geiger, *et al*. New Haven, Conn.: Human Relations
            Area Files. pp. 264-359.
1963   *The Caucasus: An Ethno-Historical Survey*. Studia
            Caucasica. 1:1-47.
Hammel, Eugene A.
1968   *Alternative Social Structures and Ritual Relations
            in the Balkans*. Englewood Cliffs, N.J.: Prentice-Hall.
Hayriye Köy Araştırma ve Planlama Çalışması
1963   Ankara: Middle East Technical University. Mimeo.
Karpat, Kemal H.
1959   *Turkey's Politics: The Transition to a Multi-Party
            System*. Princeton: Princeton University Press.
1973   "Social Groups and the Political System after 1960."
            In *Social Change and Politics in Turkey: A Structural-
            Historical Analysis*. K. H. Karpat, *et al.*, Leiden: E.J.
            Brill. pp. 227-281.
Kazamias, Andreas M.
1966   *Education and the Quest for Modernity in Turkey*.
            Chicago: University of Chicago Press.
Keleş, Ruşen
1972   *Urbanization in Turkey*. New York: An International
            Urbanization Survey Report to the Ford Foundation.
1976   "Investment by Turkish Migrants in Real Estate."
            In *Turkish Workers in Europe 1960-1975*. Nermin
            Abadan-Unat, *et al.*, Leiden: E.J. Brill. pp. 169-178.
Kiray, Mübeccel Belik
1968   "Some Notes on Elected Headmen and Mayors in
            Different Communities in Turkey." In *Local Government
            and National Development*. Ankara: Institute of Public
            Administration for Turkey and the Middle East. pp.
            113-117.
1976   "The Family of the Immigrant Worker." In *Turkish
            Workers in Europe 1960-1975*. Nermin Abadan-Unat,
            et al., Leiden: E.J. Brill. pp. 210-234.
Kirby, Fay
1960   *The Village Institute Movement of Turkey: An
            Educational Mobilization for Social Change*. Unpublish-
            ed Ph.D. dissertation. Teachers College, Columbia
            University.

Kırzıoğlu, Fahrettin M.
1953   *Kars Tarihi.* Volume I. Istanbul: Işil Matbassı.
Kolars, John F.
1963   *Tradition, Season, and Change in a Turkish Village.*
              University of Chicago Department of Geography
              Research Paper No. 82.
Koşay, Hamit Z.
1932   *Anadilden Derlemeler.* Istanbul: Ishak Refet Matbassı.
Krane, Ronald E.
1975   "Effects of International Migration upon Occupational
              Mobility, Acculturation and the Labor Market in
              Turkey." In *Manpower Mobility across Cultural
              Boundaries.* R.E. Krane, Ed. Leiden: E.J. Brill. pp.
              161-204.
Kroeber, Alfred
1948   *Anthropology.* New York: Harcourt, Brace and Co.
Kuipers, Aert H.
1956a   "Ethnic Groups." In *The Caucasus.* Volume I. Bernhard
              Geiger, *et al.,* New Haven, Conn.: Human Relations Area
              Files. pp. 377-402.
1956b   "Social Structure." In *The Caucasus.* Volume II.
              Bernhard Geiger, *et al.,* New Haven, Conn.: Human
              Relations Area Files. pp. 526-541.
Kunkel, John H.
1970   *Society and Economic Growth: A Behavioral Perspective
              of Social Change.* New York: Oxford University Press.
Lang, David Marshall
1962   *A Modern History of Soviet Georgia.* New York:
              Grove Press.
Lévi-Strauss, Claude
1966   *The Savage Mind.* Chicago: University of Chicago
              Press.
Lewis, W. Arthur
1965   "Beyond African Dictatorship." *Encounter* 25:2:3-18
Linn, Erwin L.
1966   "Reference Group: A Case Study of Conceptual
              Diffusion." *Sociological Quarterly* 7:489-499.
Lopreato, Joseph
1967   *Peasants No More.* San Francisco: Chandler.
Luzbetak, Louis J.
1951   *Marriage and the Family in Caucasia.* Vienna:
              St. Gabriel's Press.

Magnarella, Paul J.
1973   "The Reception of Swiss Family Law in Turkey."
        Anthropological Quarterly 46:2:100-116.
1974   *Tradition and Change in a Turkish Town.* Cambridge
        MA: Schenkman/John Wiley and Sons.
1976   "The Assimilation of Georgians in Turkey: A Case
        Study." *The Muslim World* 66:1:35-43.
Magnarella, Paul J., and Orhan Türkdoğan
1973   "Descent, Affinity, and Ritual Relations in Eastern
        Turkey." *American Anthropologist* 75:5:1626-1633.
Makal, Mahmut
1954   *A Village in Anatolia.* Wyndham Deedes, Trans.
        London: Vallentine, Mitchell and Co.
Malinowski, Bronislaw
1962   *Sex, Culture, and Myth.* New York: Harcourt, Brace,
        and World.
Meadows, Donella H., *et al.*
1974   *The Limits to Growth.* New York: Universe Books.
        2nd. ed.
Menges, Karl H.
1956   "Geographical Setting." In *The Caucasus.* Volume I.
        Bernhard Geiger, *et al.* New Haven, Conn.: Human
        Relations Area Files. pp. 17-263.
Merton, Robert K.
1957   *Social Theory and Social Structure.* Glencoe: The
        Free Press. Revised ed.
Mintz, Sidney W., and Eric R. Wolf
1950   "An Analysis of Ritual Co-Parenthood" (Compadrazgo).
        Southwestern Journal of Anthropology 6:341-368.
Modernization in Turkish Villages
1974   Ankara: Turkish Republic State Planning Organization,
        Pub. No. SPO:1335 - SPD:262.
Moore, Sally Falk
1973   "Law and Social Change: The Semi-autonomous Social
        Field as an Appropriate Subject of Study." *Law and
        Society Review* 7:4:719-746.
Mosak, Harold H., and Rudolf Dreikurs
1973   "Adlerian Psychotherapy." In *Current Psychotherapies.
        Raymond Corsini, Ed. Itasca, Ill.: F.E. Peacock, pp.
        35-83.*
Muin, Muhammed-i
1342 A.H.   *Burhan-i Gati.* Volume III. Tehran: Ibni
        Sina Kitabevi.

Murphy, Gardner
1947   *Personality: A Biosocial Approach to Origins and Structure.* New York: Harper.

Ornek, Sedat Veyis
1971   *Anadolu Folklorunda Ölüm.* Ankara: Ankara University Press.

Ozguner, Orhan
1970   *Köyde Mimari Doğu Karadeniz.* Ankara: Middle East Technical University Faculty of Architecture Pub. No. 13.

Ozkan (Melaşvili), Ahmet
1968   *Gürcüstan: Tarih, Edebiyat, Sanat, Folklor.* Istanbul: Aksiseda Matbaası.

Payaslioğlu, Arif T.
1964   "Political Leadership and Political Parties: Turkey." In *Political Modernization in Japan and Turkey.* R.E. Ward and D.A. Rustow, Eds. Princeton: Princeton University Press. pp. 411-433.

Penninx, R., and L. van Velzen
1976   "Evaluation of Migrants' Investment and Their Effects on Development in Boğazlıyan District." In *Migration and Development.* Nermin Abadan-Unat, *et al.,* Ankara: Ajans-Türk Press. pp. 291-325.

Peristiany, J.G., Ed.
1966   *Honour and Shame: The Values of Mediterranean Society.* Chicago: University of Chicago Press.

Peters, Emrys. L.
1963   "Aspects of Rank and Status among Muslims in a Lebanese Village." In *Mediterranean Countrymen.* J. Pitt-Rivers, Ed. The Hague: Mouton.

Philpott, Stuart B.
1970   "The Implications of Migration for Sending Societies: Some Theoretical Considerations." In *Migration and Anthropology.* R.F. Spencer, Ed. Seattle: American Ethnological Society/University of Washington Press. pp. 9-20

Potter, Jack M., *et al.* Eds.
1967   *Peasant Society: A Reader.* Boston: Little, Brown and Co.

Quarterly Economic Review
1976   "Turkey." No. 1.

Radcliffe-Brown, A.R.
1948   *The Adaman Islanders.* Glencoe, Ill.: The Free Press.
Redfield, Robert
1956   *Peasant Society and Culture.* Chicago: University
            of Chicago Press.
Renselaar, H. van, and L. van Velzen
1976   "Public and Private Initiatives Aimed at Using
            External Labour Emigration for Development." In
            Migration and Development. Nermin Abadan-Unat,
            et al., Ankara: Ajans-Turk Press. pp. 99-137.
Robakidzé, A.I.
1963   "Habitation et Villages des Montagnards de la
            Georgie dans le Passe et de Nos Jours." *Bedi
            Kartlisa* 15-16:43-44:58-62.
Robbins, Richard H.
1973   "Identity, Culture, and Behavior." In *Handbook of
            Social and Cultural Anthropology.* John J. Honigmann,
            Ed. Chicago: Rand McNally. pp. 1199-1222.
Robinson, Richard D.
1949   *Village Law.* Letter 24. Institute of Current World
            Affairs. New York.
Rogers, Everett M.
1969   *Modernization among Peasants.* New York: Holt,
            Rinehart and Winston.
Rustow, Dankwart A.
1957   "Politics and Islam in Turkey 1920-1925." In *Islam
            and the West.* Richard N. Frey, Ed. 'S-Gravenhage:
            Mouton. pp. 69-107.
Schmitt, Raymond
1972   *The Reference Other Orientation.* Carbondale, Ill.:
            Southern Illinois University Press.
Scott, Richard B.
1968   *The Village Headman in Turkey: A Case Study.* Ankara:
            Institute of Public Administration for Turkey and the
            Middle East.
Shanin, Teodor, Ed.
1971   *Peasants and Peasant Society.* Middlesex and Baltimore:
            Penguin Books.
1973   "Peasantry: Delineation of a Sociological Concept
            and a Field of Study." *Peasant Studies Newsletter*
            2:1:1-8.

Sherif, Muzafer and Carolyn W. Sherif
    1969   *Social Psychology.* New York: Harper and Row.
Sherwood, W.B.
    1967   "The Rise of the Justice Party in Turkey." *World Politics* 20: 1:54-65.
Shils, Edward A.
    1961   "Centre and Periphery." In *The Logic of Personal Knowledge: Essays Presented to Michael Polanyi.* Glencoe, Ill.: The Free Press. pp. 117-130.
Silverman, Sydel F.
    1968   "Agricultural Organization, Social Structure, and Values in Italy: Amoral Familism Reconsidered." *American Anthropologist* 70:1:1-20
Simić, Andrie
    1975   *The Ethnology of Traditional and Complex Societies.* AAAS Study Guides on Contemporary Problems. (Test Ed.)
Stirling, Paul
    1965   *Turkish Village.* New York: John Wiley and Sons.
Stycos, J. Mayone
    1965   "The Potential Role of Turkish Village Opinion Leaders in a Program of Family Planning." *Public Opinion Quarterly* 29:1:120-130.
Suttles, Gerald D.
    1972   *The Social Construction of Communities.* Chicago: University of Chicago Press.
Szyliowicz, Joseph S.
    1966   *Political Change in Rural Turkey: Erdemli.* The Hague: Mouton.
Tachau, Frank
    1972   "The Republic of Turkey." In *The Middle East: Its Government and Politics.* A.A. Al-Marayati, Ed. Belmont, Calif.: Duxbury Press.
Tannous, Afif I.
    1942   "Group Behavior in the Village Community of Lebanon." *American Journal of Sociology* 48:2:231-239.
Turner, Victor
    1967   *The Forest of Symbols.* Ithaca, N.Y.: Cornell University Press.

Wolf, Eric R.
1966   *Peasants.* Englewood Cliffs, N.J.: Prentice-Hall.
Woodworth, R.S.
1934   *Psychology.* New York: Holt. 3rd Ed.
Yasa, Ibrahim
1955   *Hasanoğlan Köyü'nün Içtimai-Iktisadi Yapısı.* Ankara: Türkiye ve Orta Doğu Amme Idaresi Enstitüsü.
Yenisey, L.
1976   "The Social Effects of Migrant Labour on the District Left Behind: Observations in Two Villages of Boğazlıyan." In *Migration and Development.* Nermin Abadan-Unat, *et al.,* Ankara: Ajans-Turk Press. pp. 327-370.